OUR LOST DECLARATION

ALSO BY SENATOR MIKE LEE

Our Lost Constitution:
The Willful Subversion of America's Founding Document

Written Out of History:
The Forgotten Founders Who Fought Big Government

SENATOR
MIKE LEE

OUR LOST DECLARATION

America's Fight Against Tyranny
from King George to the Deep State

SENTINEL

Sentinel
An imprint of Penguin Random House LLC
penguinrandomhouse.com

Most Sentinel books are available at a discount when purchased in quantity for sales promotions or corporate use. Special editions, which include personalized covers, excerpts, and corporate imprints, can be created when purchased in large quantities. For more information, please call (212) 572-2232 or e-mail specialmarkets@penguinrandomhouse.com. Your local bookstore can also assist with discounted bulk purchases using the Penguin Random House corporate Business-to-Business program. For assistance in locating a participating retailer, e-mail B2B@penguinrandomhouse.com.

Library of Congress Cataloging-in-Publication Data

Names: Lee, Mike, 1971– author.
Title: Our lost declaration : America's fight against tyranny from King George
    to the deep state / Mike Lee.
Description: New York : Sentinel, 2019. |
Identifiers: LCCN 2019003127 (print) | LCCN 2019004371 (ebook) |
    ISBN 9780525538578 (ebook) | ISBN 9780525538554 (hardback)
Subjects: LCSH: United States. Declaration of Independence. | United States--History--
    Revolution, 1775-1783. | United States--Politics and government. | BISAC: HISTORY
    / United States / Revolutionary Period (1775-1800). | HISTORY / United States /
    General. | POLITICAL SCIENCE / Government / General.
Classification: LCC E221 (ebook) | LCC E221 .L434 2019 (print) | DDC 973.3/13--dc23
LC record available at https://lccn.loc.gov/2019003127

Printed in the United States of America
10 9 8 7 6 5 4 3 2 1

To James, John, and Eliza

CONTENTS

AUTHOR'S NOTE

Readers of my last two books will be familiar with my style of trying to bring the past to life in a way that actively engages readers beyond simply reciting facts. In some cases, this means taking some dramatic license with specific incidents or conversations. This project involved extensive research, and although the final product stays true to the facts and the vision of history that resulted from that research, some elements have been discreetly added to scene descriptions to bring them into fuller resolution for the reader. We may not know, for instance, exactly what words passed between Thomas Truxtun and Captain William Garnier of HMS *Argo*, but we know they encountered each other in the Caribbean, and why not give some life to what must surely have been a rousing high-seas adventure?

We twenty-first-century Americans are extremely fortunate, too, that so many primary sources from the tumultuous days of our founding have not only survived, but also been digitized and made available for all to view. Thanks to these considerable resources, it has been possible to include dialogue drawn from contemporary accounts in a number of instances, making the scenes as true to life as possible. To all of the organizations and individuals involved in that important work of cataloguing and digitizing these early American documents and resources, I extend a special thanks.

PREFACE

WE HEAR A LOT ABOUT THE DESPERATE STATE OF AMERICAN society today. The news is full of stories of divisions at home and interference from abroad and talk of indictment and impeachment. If you listen to the media, you might think America is falling apart.

These certainly are times that try the souls of nations (to paraphrase Thomas Paine, about whom we will hear much more in this book). Yet despite the challenges and controversies of the day, our nation can continue to thrive. Our system has held up miraculously well for more than two hundred years—making the United States the oldest-existing nation with a constitutional government in which we, the people, elect our own leader and representatives.

Much of that success is due to the foundations of our law in the U.S. Constitution. I never stop marveling at the genius of the Constitution; that's why after law school, I went into business to defend it: as an assistant U.S. attorney in Salt Lake City, as a law clerk for Samuel Alito (today a Supreme Court justice), and currently as a member of the U.S. Senate and its Judiciary Committee.

After everything I've witnessed in these roles, I remain confident that our system of government protects people better than any other system of government the world has seen.

And yet, as much as we should all strive to preserve, protect, and defend our Constitution, the American system relies on more than the mechanics of government outlined in that document—three coequal branches, separation of powers, and the like—to keep the country functioning. What gives life to that system is our animating spirit, readily apparent in the Constitution's preamble but which was more fully articulated eleven years before, in the Declaration of Independence.

The Declaration is certainly appreciated but too often not fully understood. Scores of students are busily engaged in the study of constitutional law, but who studies "Declaration law"? There are legitimate reasons for this imbalance, of course. For one thing, the Declaration is significantly shorter than the Constitution, clocking in at only 1,337 of (mostly) Thomas Jefferson's words. And technically speaking, the Declaration is not a legal document—it does not set out a legal code or contain the building blocks for a system of government. Its purpose is far simpler—and perhaps even more prescient.

Jefferson details, in clear and often indignant language, all the various outrages that King George III committed against his own subjects, who just happened to live on the wrong side of the Atlantic Ocean. Just governance, as British subjects understood it, was indeed falling apart. The Declaration's signers saw plainly that the decisions made by His Majesty's Government violated their natural rights to life, liberty, and property—rights that would have been upheld had they been living in Britain.

Moreover, as colonists with no representation in Parliament, our Founders and their forebears had no way to give their consent to be governed. Equal protection of rights and the consent of the governed . . . a simple set of principles, which proclaimed to the world a new nation which was, in the words of a great American of a later generation, "conceived in liberty, and dedicated to the proposition that all men are created equal."

This was an unprecedented origin story for a country, and the Declaration of Independence was an unprecedented document. The truth that "all men are created equal" was so simple as to be "self-evident," the Declaration stated (although, as we will also see, these were not Jefferson's original words). Also self-evident was the truth that all were "endowed by their Creator with certain unalienable Rights, that among these are Life, Liberty and the pursuit of Happiness."

That "spirit of 1776"—enshrining (albeit not fully achieving) the concepts of equal rights before the law and rejecting tyrannical government—gave birth to a truly exceptional nation. It has grown into a nation that has stamped out totalitarianism around the world and remains a beacon of hope for those in search of a better life.

But I worry that too many of us—including those who serve in government—are losing that spirit. We are becoming unmoored from the Declaration's ideals, flailing in the deep waters of our unnavigable regulatory state, an insatiable centralized government, and the winds of judicial activism—the tyrannical tendencies that rear their heads today. When American citizens can be hauled in front of administrative law judges for abiding by their honest religious convictions, as happened to baker Jack Phillips in Colorado in 2013, are all of our rights really as safe as we think?

What inspired our Founders in those first tumultuous years as thirteen colonies fought for recognition as united states? Their desire to never return to a monarchical system in which they were subject to the whims of a king and a powerful central government that acted in His Majesty's name. Indeed, this is why the bulk of the Declaration of Independence is taken up with detailing just what King George III had done that his former subjects found intolerable. And in reading this most significant, often-overlooked section of the Declaration today, one is struck by how timely so many of these grievances sound. Consider the following excerpts:

"He has refused his Assent to Laws, the most wholesome and necessary for the public good." When a president fails to enforce the law on the books or does so in bad faith because of political disagreements, he damages the public good.

"He has erected a multitude of New Offices, and sent hither swarms of Officers to harrass our people, and eat out their substance." Today, a massive regulatory state manned by "swarms" of unelected bureaucrats continues to harass our citizens with burdensome federal red tape.

"For suspending our own Legislatures, and declaring themselves invested with power to legislate for us in all cases whatsoever." The individual legislatures of individual states have today been all but suspended in practice, as a flawed understanding of federalism allows for the creeping centralization of power in the hands of the federal government in Washington, DC.

Many of the problems the American colonists experienced with King George are, either directly or indirectly, still with us today. This is a consequence of a federal bureaucracy that has been allowed to expand under both Republican and Democratic presidents. It gathers more power however it can, stripping that power away from states, localities, and ultimately the people—contrary to the Founders' intent.

Jefferson warned us about the dangers of centralized, overreaching power in the Declaration, and by heeding these warnings today, we might be able to stop the march of government expansion. What if rediscovering the Declaration of Independence—even more than the Constitution—is the key to returning America to a land of limited government, individual rights, and personal freedom? Because if we actually adhered to the spirit of the Declaration of Independence, we would have an improved state of affairs today.

In 1790, upon visiting a synagogue in Rhode Island, George Washington wrote to the Jewish worshippers that in this new nation, "all possess alike liberty of conscience and immunities of citizenship." No longer were they subjects of a monarch whose personal biases—religious or otherwise—outweighed their dignity as beings created equal. "It is now no more that toleration is spoken of," Washington wrote, "as if it was by the indulgence of one class of people, that another enjoyed the exercise of their inherent natural rights."[1]

Nine years later, George Washington would pass away at his home of Mount Vernon, a plantation on which he lived and worked—with 317 human beings held as property. Washington's will declared that all the slaves owned legally by him—123 in all—would be freed after his wife, Martha, died. Despite this virtuous last act, an acknowledgment of the injustice of slavery,

Washington and his fellow slave-owning Founders still perpetu-
ated a system that violated the unalienable rights of others. Realizing the ideals in the Declaration of Independence would turn
out to be a very long, bloody process—and there still remains work
to be done.

This is something I can understand on a very personal level. I
know it may seem strange—as a white male U.S. senator, what do
I know about having your rights taken away? The answer has to do
with the reason I serve in the Senate as an elected official from
Utah and not, say, from New York or Illinois.

I'm a member of the Church of Jesus Christ of Latter-day
Saints, as are many of my Utah constituents. We Mormons didn't
end up in Utah because everyone got the same coupon in the mail.
Mormon pioneers, including my ancestors, moved west because
they were banished from everywhere else they tried to live. The
church had its beginnings in New York, but its members kept
moving westward to Ohio, then to Missouri, then to Illinois, and
finally to Utah—often one step ahead of an angry mob that was
dead set against living in harmony with this faith. And these
weren't simple disputes among neighbors. The discrimination
against Mormons came from the top down. On October 27, 1838,
Missouri governor Lilburn Boggs issued an executive order stating, "The Mormons must be treated as enemies, and must be
exterminated or driven from the State if necessary, for the public
peace."

A sitting U.S. governor called for some of his people to be
"exterminated" simply by virtue of the faith they practiced. This
would seem to fly in the face of the protection of "unalienable
Rights" that the Declaration guarantees. The "unalienable Rights"

of the Missouri Mormons to "Life, Liberty and the pursuit of Happiness" were certainly not "self-evident" to Governor Boggs.

The Declaration can be ignored, perverted, and even trampled on by those who happen to temporarily hold power. We need to remain vigilant against abuses of that power even today. And there is no more powerful rebuke of overweening, centralized power than that document penned by Thomas Jefferson in 1776.

This book is a reexamination of the Declaration of Independence that aims to restore its rightful place alongside the Constitution. I hope you will be convinced of its fundamental importance to our country's foundation and awed, as I am, by its prescient wisdom.

INTRODUCTION
The Search for Unalienable Rights

A SEVEN-YEAR-OLD NEW YORK BOY'S LEMONADE STAND GETS shut down by overzealous health inspectors. In Colorado, a cake baker gets his business shut down and protested because he refuses to design a cake celebrating a gay wedding because it violates his deeply held Christian belief that marriage is between a man and a woman. Federal regulatory agencies get to police themselves and tell those of us in Congress charged with their oversight to shove off because of an obscure 1984 Supreme Court case, *Chevron v. Natural Resources Defense Council.* U.S. taxpayers are paying for a foreign war in Yemen that their elected representatives never voted to pursue, much like colonial Americans were dragooned into fighting the French at His Majesty's Government's direction. Administrative law judges wield singular judicial power over Americans who are subject to proceedings without a jury of their peers.

Usurpations of our rights happen every day in America, with barely any notice by those who claim to be champions of rights. Listen to progressives like Bernie Sanders or Alexandria Ocasio-Cortez talk. It's an amazing thing. They've co-opted the language of our Founding Fathers by speaking of "rights." We have "rights," and we're entitled to them, the progressive Left tells us. A "right" to universal health care, a "right" to free higher education, a "right" to a guaranteed living wage, a "right" to kill the unborn, a "right" to switch genders. And so on.

Are these actually "rights"? Put a different way, are these the same "rights" that conservatives believe in? As with so many other concepts which the progressive Left latches onto, the concept of "rights" has been so perverted by them that it bears little resemblance to the idea of "rights" as the founding generation of Americans understood them—the "rights" they fought for and preserved in our founding documents. Those rights were designed to protect the individual against aggression from others and especially, in the eyes of the Founders, aggression from their government. The rights weren't gifts to be bestowed on citizens by government but rather a statement that the citizens had those rights conferred by nature and by God. Government's primary job was to ensure that those rights were not infringed.

For the first time in the annals of human history, the Declaration of Independence set out exactly what "unalienable rights" are. Our utter lack of knowledge about those rights is directly responsible for the growth of big government, in the form of both an unaccountable "deep-state" bureaucracy and the progressive politicians who think they can win their way into office by promising more government handouts than the next one and cloaking those handouts in the guise of "rights."

The Left's so-called rights are destroying lives, eroding liberty, and making it harder to pursue happiness every day in America.

It's not just that the Left's "rights" are anathema to the true meaning of the word. It's that their "rights," by their very nature, usurp the rights of others. When governments grant collective rights, they erode individual rights, which in the United States are known as "negative rights." When a central government administers a sprawling health care program, for instance, it ends up coercing its citizens by taking both their liberty and property. The truth is it's still happening today, and we must be ever vigilant against a government— even with one branch led by a Republican or conservative—that encroaches on our rights.

But while the political Left grows more energized than it has been in generations, conservatives grow complacent. We've lost sight of what we are really fighting for beyond easy talking points like "conservative judges," "lower taxes," "less regulation." We agree those are good things. But *why* are they good things? *Why, after all, do we call ourselves "conservatives"? What exactly are we conserving?*

Our failure to answer those questions (and, let's face it, even to ask them in the first place) is why we are still in danger of losing not only the "culture war" but also the hearts and minds of an entire generation of young Americans. It's why a near majority of millennials, according to surveys, would rather live in a socialist economy than a capitalist one and vote overwhelmingly for liberals. It's also why we lose elections. It's why we lost the House of Representatives in 2018. It's why we could lose the presidency in 2020. And the stakes then will likely be even higher than they were in 2016. We're not looking at a Hillary Clinton–like figure, who despite her liberal bona fides is an establishment Democrat and always sides with Goldman Sachs and Davos over Occupy

Wall Street and Code Pink. We're now looking at a Democratic Party intent on nominating the most liberal candidate for president in American history—an Elizabeth Warren, Bernie Sanders, Kamala Harris, or Robert "Beto" O'Rourke.

Should a candidate like this win the nomination and then the presidency, our future is almost certainly one of single-payer socialist health care, sky-high tax rates, and a federal government that funds everything from abortions at any time for any reason to elective surgeries for minors who identify as a different gender. It's a sobering thought, and one we need to come to terms with rather than simply wish it away or pretend it will never happen here.

This steady growth of government began in the United States in the early twentieth century, received massive boosts in the 1930s and 1960s, and has continued into the new millennium. The phenomenon has gone by many names. In its first years, it was branded "progressivism" by early adopters like Woodrow Wilson. Certain expansionist programs had their own catchy names, like Franklin Roosevelt's "New Deal" or Lyndon Johnson's "Great Society." Those who took a more skeptical view of unchecked government expansion (no matter how lofty the stated purpose)—among whose ranks I include myself—used different terms. It could simply be called "big government," or the "administrative state," or even the "deep state."

No matter the name, the problem is consistent: There are millions of government personnel exercising powers over "the governed" to which they did not consent. Thomas Jefferson, as he so often did, had an apt phrase for this. In the Declaration, he charged that King George had "erected a multitude of new offices, and sent hither swarms of officers to harrass our people, and eat out their substance." Well, the "swarms of officers" are gathering once again—but they're not in London; they're in Washington.

Over the last century, the administrative, or deep, state has grown to inordinate size and power. This growth has continued under presidents of both political parties, though some actively encourage it while others make valiant efforts to stop it. That's one of the most insidious qualities of the administrative state—it can perpetuate itself no matter who is nominally supervising it. It's like a monster that continues to live and breathe and grow no matter who is supposed to be guarding it. The government outlined by our Founders, which received its earliest articulation in the Declaration of Independence, has grown unchecked to the point where a powerful central government is once again exercising outsize power and influence over the American people—except this time it's of our own making.

Which brings us to why I wrote this book. Generally, those of us who call ourselves conservatives are the ones who want to keep government small, to prevent the growth of the administrative state. But what does that really mean, especially in an era where outright socialism—and the massive government expansion it entails—is becoming increasingly popular in the mainstream American political conversation? Our complacency is tantamount to consent!

Good governments, the Declaration points out, exist in a system in which they are "deriving their just powers from the consent of the governed." And how do "the governed" exercise their influence over the government?

There are a number of ways that the people give the consent by which the government derives its just powers: They elect representatives in Congress who use their powers of funding and oversight as a check against the executive branch; the executive branch itself is headed by an elected president, who then appoints people to supervise other parts of the government in ways that are consistent with his or her mandate; Supreme Court justices are appointed by the elected president to interpret the law and make sure the rest of the government is functioning within the boundaries of the Constitution. This is how it is supposed to work, at least in theory.

The problem is that in practice, a government—even one set up with the best of intentions—can become so large and convoluted that it ends up wielding some powers *without* that all-important "consent of the governed." Instead of "just powers," its powers become unjust. And before you know it, millions of unelected bureaucrats are handling much of the day-to-day business of government through a tangled web of executive branch agencies.

The administrative state looms large as a presence in the affairs of too many Americans. Its influence creeps into our lives, holding sway over our families, our businesses, and our lands. By operating through this deep state, government is able to avoid being accountable to the citizens whom it is supposed to serve—to you and me.

The grassroots movement known as the Tea Party that came to prominence in 2009 helped spark a widespread national rediscovery of our Constitution. And yet, I'm convinced that too many of us—then and now—neglected the Constitution's older sister, the Declaration of Independence. That spirit of 1776 is what is missing in our civic life today.

We hold these truths to be self-evident, that all men are created equal, that they are endowed by their Creator with certain unalienable Rights, that among these are Life, Liberty and the pursuit of Happiness.

These words were written by a Virginian named Thomas Jefferson. He was a man who embodied all the advantages, faults, and contradictions of his era. He was a brilliant thinker and inventor who had time to think and invent because enslaved people worked his land and made his money for him. He wrote "all men are created equal" at a moment when, across the British colonies and even at his estate at Monticello, that statement wasn't exactly self-evident for scores of African Americans who lived in bondage.

Just as powerful in that sentence as Jefferson's bold statement of equality was the listing of inalienable (or in earlier drafts, "unalienable") rights, rights that no government can take away from individuals. Never before had these ideas been expressed in such a concise form.

And yet, for all the earth-shattering revelation contained within Jefferson's simple sentence and the rest of the relatively short document in which it is found, we—as modern heirs to its teachings—do not fully appreciate its gravity. Sadly, this phenomenon is both demonstrable and quantifiable.

A survey taken shortly after the turn of the twenty-first century found that more than 40 percent of Americans could not name Thomas Jefferson as the author of the Declaration of Independence.[1] Another poll a few years later found that more than a quarter of us could not name Great Britain as the country from which that independence was declared.[2]

An even more disheartening expression of our lack of familiarity with the Declaration came in the summer of 2017. To celebrate the Fourth of July that year, National Public Radio's Twitter account tweeted out the entirety of the Declaration—line by line, word by word. The reaction of a number of Twitter users was surprising, to say the least.

When NPR tweeted America's grievances against King George III as listed in the Declaration—which acknowledged that he "obstructed the administration of justice" and concluded that "a Prince whose character is thus marked by every act which may define a Tyrant, is unfit to be the ruler of a free people"—some on Twitter thought the broadcaster was talking about a very different leader: President Donald Trump. They misinterpreted Jefferson's words from 1776 as a rallying cry for insurrection today.

"So, NPR is calling for revolution," one Twitter user wrote. Another blasted the outlet for tweeting "propaganda."[3] There was, of course, a notable commonality among the Twitter accounts that were so quick to take NPR to task—most of them appeared to belong to conservatives.

Conservatives might be forgiven for thinking NPR was out to get President Trump. That particular news organization is not known for erring on the side of generosity when it comes to giving fair coverage to right-of-center beliefs and those who express them. Perhaps the controversy ginned up by NPR's seemingly innocuous—even patriotic—tweeting says more about our current social-media outrage culture than it does about any particular ideology.

In 2018, Facebook removed a post from a Texas newspaper

that posted sections of the Declaration of Independence. The post went "against our standards on hate speech," Facebook explained. The fact remains that Americans of all political persuasions should know the words of the Declaration of Independence when they see them. They should be studied, consulted for counsel and guidance, and cherished to ensure they will be passed down to the next generation. The most disrespectful thing we can do to the Declaration of Independence is to take it (and the principles underlying it) for granted. Regrettably, that's what many of us seem to be doing.

Perhaps the saddest statistic about America's knowledge of the Declaration is this one, from 2013: At that time, more than 70 percent of Americans thought the men who pledged "their lives, their fortunes, and their sacred honor" by signing the Declaration would not be proud of how the America they fought for had turned out.[4]

A few dozen intelligent men who lived on the edge of a vast wilderness 250 years ago understood the dangers of vast centralized power. While they were busy living, working, praying, and building a vibrant civilization, a monarch thousands of miles away and the government that acted in his name began chipping away at their rights—taxing them without their consent, boarding soldiers in their homes, imprisoning friends and family members for expressing their opinions. The grievances against a tyrannical King George in the eighteenth century increasingly bear a striking resemblance to the capricious actions of an out-of-control federal government today.

Fortunately, back then there were patriots who knew that

unless they led a revolution on behalf of the rights of the individual against their government, the future of human history wouldn't be too different from the past—it would remain a brutal story of rulers taking advantage of the ruled. And so they got to work. Under penalty of treason and death, they put their names on a document that changed the world.

CHAPTER ONE

"In General Congress Assembled"

We were all in haste; Congress was impatient and
the Instrument was reported, as I believe in Jefferson's hand writing as he first drew it.

—JOHN ADAMS, 1822

STATE HOUSE, PHILADELPHIA
July 3, 1776

THE HEAT WAS RISING INSIDE THE PENNSYLVANIA STATE HOUSE,
in almost every conceivable way. The hot summer sun beat
down upon the building, threatening to bake the clay bricks of the
outer wall a second time over. Inside, the air was warm, muggy, and
stagnant. Flies buzzed about the debating chamber, forcing the
delegates to the Continental Congress assembled therein to shoo
them away with hands and handkerchiefs, as if they were punctuat-
ing their remarks with even more hand gestures than usual.

Their talk was getting heated as well. Since the first of the month they had been debating the document submitted by the committee appointed to draft it, known as the Committee of Five. The principal author was Thomas Jefferson of Virginia. Jefferson's draft had already gone through a number of revisions by his fellow committee members, particularly at the hands of John Adams and Benjamin Franklin. Now the entire membership of the Continental Congress was having a go at what would become the opening statement of a new era. All of them were conscious of this document's significance, and before it was approved, the full Congress wanted to make sure every sentence, every word, was exactly right. They knew that history demanded nothing less of them. And perhaps some of them—being politicians, after all—were anxious to make sure Jefferson's draft bore *their* fingerprints as well.

Meanwhile, the paper's principal author sat sullenly on the sidelines of the debate. Jefferson himself did not engage in the discussion but was rather, in his own recollection, "writhing a little under the acrimonious criticisms" leveled by some of his colleagues.[1] To a writer of such great passion as Jefferson, it was no doubt disheartening to see and hear how his words were being tweaked, prodded, rearranged, and replaced by others.

While most of his fellow delegates were single-mindedly engaged with the editing at hand, Jefferson's obvious discomfort did not escape the notice of Benjamin Franklin. As a member of the Committee of Five and, along with Adams, one of the first to review Jefferson's work, Franklin had been responsible for some modest changes of his own. But now that Jefferson's work had been cast before the whole boisterous Congress, Franklin could see that the Virginian was taking the criticism hard.

At seventy years old, Franklin was the oldest member of the

Continental Congress. He felt that his young, talented, but sensitive, friend might benefit from some of the wisdom that came with age. The old Philadelphian, his gray hair down to his shoulders, moving slowly on account of gout, shuffled over to Jefferson and sat down next to him.

"I have made it a rule," he told Jefferson, "whenever in my power, to avoid becoming the draughtsman of papers to be reviewed by a public body."

Both men knew it was a little late for that advice, but Franklin continued apace: "I took my lesson from an incident which I will relate to you." Whether Jefferson in his editorial agony wanted to hear it or not, a story was coming.

"When I was a journeyman printer," Franklin began, "one of my companions, an apprentice hatter, having served out his time, was about to open shop for himself. His first concern was to have a handsome signboard, with a proper inscription."

The friend's name was John Thompson, and Franklin explained that he sketched out an image of what his sign would look like. It included the words "John Thompson, Hatter, makes and sells hats for ready money," along with a picture of a hat. The design seemed simple enough.

"But," Franklin continued, "he thought he would submit it to his friends for their amendments." Here young John Thompson ran into trouble.

The first friend to take a look felt it unnecessary for Thompson to call himself a "Hatter" on the sign *and* to say "makes and sells hats for ready money." Anyone who read that he made and sold hats would know he was a hatter. So Thompson scratched out "Hatter" from the sketch of the sign.

A second friend suggested getting rid of the word *makes* "because," as Franklin explained, "his customers would not care who made the hats. If good and to their mind, they would buy by whomsoever made." "Makes" was thus crossed out.

Thompson's third friend offered the very practical advice of avoiding the phrase "for ready money," since it was bad business to sell hats or anything else on credit. Thompson should leave no question that his customers would have to pay, and so that phrase was similarly excised.

"The inscription," Franklin went on, "now stood 'John Thompson sells hats.' *Sells hats?* says his next friend. *Nobody will expect you to give them away! What then is the use of that word?* It was stricken out, and 'hats' followed it, the rather as there was one painted on the board.

"So," concluded Franklin, "the inscription was reduced ultimately to 'John Thompson' with the figure of a hat."[2]

With this amusing story of an eighteenth-century "branding exercise," Franklin offered some comfort to Jefferson as they watched the other members of Congress argue over the wording of the Declaration of Independence. Like John Thompson the hatter, Jefferson had entrusted his ideas to others, each of whom made their own particular mark upon the original. And like Thompson's friends, Jefferson's colleagues in Congress meant no personal affront when they offered their suggestions for improvement. Still, the changes were personally painful to Jefferson. The sting had not faded even decades later when he referred to them in 1818 as "depredations" and "mutilations" committed against his original text.[3]

One of these was the removal of especially brutal language against not just King George III but the British people altogether, whom Jefferson accused of sending "Scotch & foreign mercenaries" to the colonies—which understandably offended Continental Congress delegates of Scottish background.[4] It was true that "foreign mercenaries" had been employed in combat in America, notably soldiers hired from Germany—the ancestral home of George III—who were especially hated by the colonists thanks to their particular zeal for looting and plundering.[5]

Jefferson was so enraged that he wanted to cut all ties with the British, not just political ones, arguing that "manly spirit bids us to renounce for ever these unfeeling brethren" and "we must endeavor to forget our former love for them." This severely Anglophobic language was watered down to preserve the hope of regaining normal relations with Britain in the future, but the final word on the former mother country was still Jefferson's: We would "hold them, as we hold the rest of mankind, enemies in war, in peace friends."

In the end, John Adams recalled, "Congress cut off about a quarter" of the original Declaration and in the process "obliterated some of the best of it."[6] Historian Julian Boyd observes dryly: "That a public body would reduce rather than increase the number of words in a political document is in itself a remarkable testimony to their sagacity and ability to express themselves."[7] Usually, the fewer words there are in government documents, the better for the people.

STATE HOUSE, PHILADELPHIA
July 4, 1776

Once his fellow delegates had finished editing the Declaration, Jefferson's fellow Virginian Benjamin Harrison made the report that the document had been shaped into its final form. It was read aloud one more time, voted on, and officially adopted by the Continental Congress.

But what good was a Declaration if its message wasn't declared far and wide? As soon as the Declaration was officially adopted, the very next order of business for the Congress was to begin the process of disseminating it. Accordingly, they ordered "that the declaration be authenticated and printed" by one of the many printers to be found in Philadelphia. After that it was to "be sent to the several assemblies, conventions and committees, or councils of safety, and to the several commanding officers of the continental troops; that it be proclaimed in each of the United States, and at the head of the army."[8]

Note that as soon as the Declaration had been adopted, in its very next measure, the official records of the Congress were referring to "the United States." The colonies were no more. In addition, it was critical that the soldiers in the field fighting the King's soldiers were able to hear the Declaration too. Now they could hear an exquisite articulation of just what they were fighting for. And that fight was preparing to ramp up. On the very same day that Congress voted to adopt the Declaration, a fresh force of British troops under General William Howe completed landing operations on Staten Island in New York.

STATE HOUSE COURTYARD, PHILADELPHIA
July 8, 1776

They came from all over Philadelphia, called out of homes and shops by the bells that rang out from church steeples. It was, in the words of one account, a "warm sunshine morning" on Monday the eighth of July, as citizens gathered to hear the momentous news that had been spreading for the past few days.

The printer John Dunlop had worked through the night of the fourth to print the first official copies of the Declaration of Independence, and by Saturday the sixth it appeared on the front page of the *Pennsylvania Evening Post*.[9] So the words of the Declaration had been circulating, but they had not yet received their first official public reading. This was to take place at noon on the eighth, and it was for this singular event that the bells pealed and the crowds gathered.

The man chosen for this solemn duty was not a member of the Continental Congress, but he was no less a patriot. John Nixon was a native Philadelphian and a colonel in the militia, currently in charge of the city's defense. As such, it had been the task of Nixon and his militiamen to keep the Continental Congress safe were the King's forces to attack. Now it was Nixon's privilege to read aloud the fruits of Congress's labor for the first time.

He stood in front of the crowd assembled in the State House courtyard, held up the parchment just a few days off the press, and began to read. His voice was loud and clear enough to be heard the next block over, and the people responded with "repeated huzzas."[10] Some historians report that there were three cheers of "God bless the free states of North America!" (That has a nice ring to it, but it's probably best we stuck with "United States of America.")

Even after Colonel Nixon's reading, Philadelphia's bells continued to ring into the night. And before the celebrations were over, according to one newspaper, "our late King's coat of arms was brought from the Hall, in the State-House . . . and burned amidst the acclamations of a crowd of spectators."[11] The official symbol of King George III's rule over the former colonies was literally and figuratively consigned to the ashes.

STATE HOUSE, PHILADELPHIA
August 2, 1776

The celebrations had been over for some weeks, and an ominous silence now hung in chamber of the State House on the morning of August 2 as, one by one, the delegates of the Continental Congress filed up to formally sign their names to the Declaration of Independence. Among them was Dr. Benjamin Rush of Philadelphia, who remembered even decades later "the pensive and awful silence which pervaded the house when we were called up, one after another, to the table of the President of Congress, to subscribe what was believed by many at that time to be our own death warrants."[12]

The president of Congress was John Hancock, who had felt the King's injustice firsthand and is supposed to have signed his name extra large in order that George III might see it more clearly. This is likely, however, an entertaining fiction—Hancock probably signed in large letters simply because he signed first, as president.

There is another anecdote from that day for which we do have some documentation. Amid the "silence and gloom" that Rush remembered, Benjamin Harrison, known for his corpulent physique, made a clever remark to his more wizened colleague Elbridge Gerry. "I shall have a great advantage over you, Mr. Gerry, when we are all hung for what we are now doing," observed Harrison. "From the size and weight of my body I shall die in a few minutes, but from the lightness of your body you will dance in the air an hour or two before you are dead."[13]

There was a "transient smile" at this jibe, but soon the gravity of the moment returned. The Declaration was known to the world now, including the British. There was no turning back. And as they affixed their names to the document, these men knew that it was as good as crafting a most-wanted list for the Crown. Yet they went through with it. Why endure such risk? Because, simply put, they had had enough. His Majesty's Government had pushed them this far.

CHAPTER TWO
Weakening the People's Representatives

He has dissolved Representative Houses repeatedly,
for opposing with manly firmness his invasions on
the rights of the people.

BOSTON, MASSACHUSETTS BAY COLONY
1768

ON FEBRUARY 11, 1768, THE TOWN HOUSE IN BOSTON WAS, FOR a moment, the epicenter of rebellion.

New taxes imposed on the colonies by Parliament had gone into effect a few months earlier, in November 1767. Known as the Townshend Acts, these were another attempt by the government in London to squeeze revenue out of the American colonies after the repeal of the Stamp Act. The Stamp Act, a tax on all sorts of printed materials bearing an official royal "stamp," had been passed in 1765 but was so strenuously resisted by the American colonists on whom it was imposed that British merchants—in hopes of retaining their American business interests—successfully persuaded Parliament to repeal the law a year later.

But while the Stamp Act itself may have been struck from the books, its repeal was closely followed by the passage of the Declaratory Act, in which London made clear its view that all "colonies and plantations in America have been, are, and of right ought to be, subordinate unto, and dependent upon the imperial crown and parliament of Great Britain."[1] With the Townshend Acts of 1767, His Majesty's Government was doubling down on that premise.

These new taxes, in the words of the eminent Bostonian Samuel Adams, were nothing less than "infringements of their natural and constitutional rights; because, as they are not represented in the British Parliament, his Majesty's commons in Britain, by those Acts, grant their property without their consent."[2] In these early days when the American character was taking shape, our determination to protect our property rights was paramount. Luckily for us, that determination has remained strong.

The Townshend Acts also provided for more royal customs officers to be stationed in Boston, and Adams gave a warning about this expansion of government, observing that "officers of the Crown may be multiplied to such a degree as to become dangerous to the liberty of the people."[3]

Adams and others felt that by calling out this injustice, they were only speaking up for their rights as Englishmen, and Englishmen had a right to speak against unfair taxes. It is important to remember that in 1768, the American colonists were not interested in separation from Britain, but rather full exercise of the same rights enjoyed by the King's subjects in Britain itself. If taxes like the Townshend duties would not be tolerated by a British subject in London, why should they be tolerated by a subject who happened to live in Boston?

But His Majesty's Government took a decidedly different approach when his American subjects decided to speak their minds. Disturbing news soon arrived that the London government had enacted a policy allowing colonists suspected of treason to be hauled away to England for their trial.[4] And before this episode was over, the King's heavy hand would leave the many American colonists without any elected representation in their colonial governments at all.

———————

Anyone approaching the Town House, the seat of government in colonial Massachusetts, could have no doubt as to whose town this was. The road that led up to the building from the bustling docks was called King Street, which in 1768 meant it honored George III. To make the journey from the wharves to the Town House (known today as the Old State House) was to travel the busiest commercial thoroughfare in Boston—indeed, one of the most important trade hubs in His Majesty's North American colonies.

Boston's Long Wharf ran directly into King Street, where cargo from all corners of the world was unloaded. The British Empire depended on its supremacy at sea to maintain the trade routes that brought more wealth and power back to the mother country—not to mention its ruler—and Boston was a significant economic powerhouse on this side of the Atlantic.

A traveler walking up King Street from the wharves would walk alongside shipments of exotic cargo, such as tea from the Far East, carried in wagons or carts or on the backs of laborers, making their way to the storehouses of Boston merchants. Fish-mongers hawked their wares up and down the road. Bakers sold loaves of fresh bread to hungry sailors who had lived for months at sea on hardtack and salt pork. The local grog shops did a fair trade, too. The very cobblestones of King Street exuded commercial energy.

But to busy Bostonians, the brick edifice at the top of the road, overlooking the main public square, sat as a stark reminder of the ultimate beneficiary of their labors. Walking up King Street, one did not come to the front door of the Town House but instead to its east wall, the main feature of which was an ornate balcony in the center that looked out over the square and commanded a view of the bustling streets below. From this grand platform, the colony's governor (appointed by the King) would address His Majesty's loyal subjects gathered below, and royal proclamations would be read aloud to the public.

The powerful symbolism of royal commands being issued from on high must have been painfully obvious to the people clustered below. But as if that weren't enough, the east wall of the Town House was decorated with those incontrovertible symbols of the British throne—the lion and the unicorn. Looking up from the square, the people could see the unicorn with a crown around its neck (and that crown attached to chains) affixed to the roof to the right of the balcony. The lion, crown firmly on its head, was situated on the right. In that same arrangement, they still flank the royal coat of arms of Great Britain's sovereign today. The unicorn's head was carved looking ahead, over the roof of the building. The lion's head, however, was looking straight down, as if daring the Bostonians below to defy its might.

On the full British royal coat of arms from which these figures were taken, a motto appears beneath them, ironically in French: *Dieu et Mon Drot*, meaning "God and my right." This is a reference to the divine right of kings to rule their subjects. The King sought to convince his people that defiance should be understood as an act of rebellion not only against the Crown but also against God Himself.

Charles Townshend, chancellor of the exchequer—the head of the British treasury—was well aware that the laws bearing his name would be unpopular on the other side of the Atlantic. During debate in Parliament on the matter, Townshend quipped that "after this, I do not expect to have my statue erected in America."[5] But he didn't let that stop him and went on to declare, "England is undone if this taxation of America is given up."[6]

It was true that England was strapped for cash after the Seven Years' War against France, which ended in 1763. This began as a colonial conflict between the French and British in North America, but it soon grew into a costly global conflict between the two European powers. Several of its critical battles played out in the American colonies (where George Washington was then a young officer in His Majesty's forces). There, the conflict became known as the French and Indian War as the British colonists and their native allies were pitched into battle against French troops and *their* native allies. But as many colonists were painfully aware, this was a faraway monarch's war in which they had been forced to fight.

International conflicts were expensive, and years after the end of the war, London was still trying to refill the royal coffers. Though

Townshend himself died in September 1767, between his name-sake acts' passage in June and their implementation in November, his presence was certainly felt by the American colonists in the ensuing months. And they certainly weren't in any mood to erect statues. Thanks to Townshend, they now faced new taxes on the tea they drank, the paint on their walls, the glass in their windows, and the paper on which they wrote.[7] The Bostonians were determined to fight back, and despite the tax upon it, paper was to be their weapon.

On the second floor of Boston's Town House could be found the chamber of the Massachusetts House of Representatives, and the gentlemen gathered within it on the morning of February 11 quieted down upon hearing Speaker Thomas Cushing rap his gavel on the desk. The House had come to order at ten that morning and quickly proceeded to the second order of business on the day's docket—the item that would prove the most consequential to history.

On February 4, the House had voted to appoint a committee to draft a letter to be sent to the legislatures of all other British colonies with the intent of addressing the "difficulties" brought about by "the operation of several Acts of Parliament for levying Duties and Taxes on the American Colonies."[8] The leaders of Massachusetts were going to fight the injustices of the Townshend Acts, but they were not going to do it alone. It was time to call for support from their fellow legislators in the other colonial capitals.

The members of this committee tasked with drafting the "Circular Letter" included Speaker Cushing himself. Also among the committee's number were two of the leading lights of the revolutionary movement in Boston: James Otis and Samuel Adams. Otis had made quite a name for himself over the last few years, arguing against warrantless searches by colonial officials and publishing the pamphlet *Rights of the British Colonies* (you can read more about him in chapter 7 of my previous book, *Written Out of History: The Forgotten Founders Who Fought Big Government*). It was Otis and Adams who had argued most strongly for sending this letter despite the reluctance of some other legislators. Adams was also serving as clerk of the House of Representatives, and thus Speaker Cushing called upon him to read the draft of the letter aloud to their colleagues.

Samuel Adams stood up from his desk, parchment in hand, and looked about the chamber. He allowed himself to savor the moment. Though he read out many state papers as part of his duties as clerk, he took special pride in this one. The Circular Letter draft was primarily his own handiwork—with important edits from Otis and input from the rest of the committee.[9] He and Otis had worked for weeks to convince their fellow House members that this was the right course of action. Now the fate of their efforts hung in the words he was about to deliver to his hushed, expectant colleagues. If his words could move them, perhaps they could move others beyond their own colony.

Adams began: "The House of Representatives of this province have taken into their serious consideration the great difficulties that must accrue to themselves and their constituents by the operation of several Acts of Parliament, imposing duties and taxes on the American colonies."[10] The point was laid out clearly in the beginning—the taxes were the problem.

Now came the specific purpose of the letter: promoting inter-colonial unity on the issue. Adams noted that because this was "a subject in which every colony is deeply interested," it was only fitting that "all possible care should be taken that the representatives of the several assemblies, upon so delicate a point, should harmonize with each other." It was therefore the intention of the Massachusetts House to "communicate their mind to a sister colony, upon a common concern."[11]

Adams based his argument on the idea that the American colonists were full British subjects, and as such they had "an equitable claim to the full enjoyment of the fundamental rules of the British constitution." It was, furthermore, "an essential, unalterable right in nature, engrafted into the British constitution, as a fundamental law . . . that what a man has honestly acquired is absolutely his own, which he may freely give, but cannot be taken from him without his consent."[12]

Adams called this a "natural and constitutional right," which was being violated by the Townshend Acts.

As he wound down his reading of the Circular Letter, Adams sounded notes of humility. He humbled the observations of the Massachusetts House before the legislatures of the other colonies. "They freely submit their opinions to the judgment of others," he read, "and shall take it kind in your house to point out to them anything further that may be thought necessary." He closed with lines that would seem obsequious to us now: "This House cannot conclude, without expressing their firm confidence in the king, our common head and father, that the united and dutiful supplications of his distressed American subjects will meet with his royal and favorable acceptance."[13]

Samuel Adams took his seat to murmurs of approval from his colleagues. He and Otis had done their work well. Their letter was approved by the House, and now copies would be drawn up, signed by Speaker Cushing, and sent to the legislative chambers of Massachusetts's sister colonies.

With that accomplished, the House moved on to the next item on that morning's agenda. Samuel Adams stepped back from his temporary spotlight and settled back into his role as clerk. There were more-mundane matters to attend to. A gentleman from Rochester had petitioned the House to grant his local court permission to retry a lawsuit to which he'd been a party. His case had to be heard. The legislative business of the colony had to go on.

———

As it turned out, the colony's legislative business was stymied by the Massachusetts Circular Letter—as Adams's draft came to be called—thanks to an apoplectic reaction in London. When they got their hands on a copy of the letter in April 1768, the British authorities, according to historian Mark Puls, "viewed the circular letter as the colonies' most defiant act yet."[14] And the idea of all the colonies joining forces in opposition to Parliament was even less palatable.

Wills Hill, the Earl of Hillsborough, then serving as secretary of state for the colonies, flew into a rage and dashed off official instructions to the royal governors in America in an attempt to cut off the Circular Letter's influence. To the governors of the twelve other colonies, he wrote that the message from Massachusetts was "of a most dangerous and factious tendency" and would "inflame the minds" of the colonists. "You will therefore," he ordered, "exert your utmost influence to prevail upon the assembly of your province to take no notice of it, which will be treating it with the contempt it deserves." But if any of the other colonial legislatures *did* act in support of Massachusetts, Hillsborough ordered their governors "to prevent any proceedings upon it by an immediate prorogation or dissolution."[15] The people's elected representative bodies were to be disbanded if they dared take up this letter.

In his letter to Governor Francis Bernard of Massachusetts, Hillsborough provided more detail. He reported that the King deigned to give the Massachusetts colonists the benefit of the doubt. His Majesty, according to Hillsborough, felt that the Circular Letter might be "contrary to the sense of the assembly, and procured by surprise." He would give his wayward subjects a chance to set things right. Bernard was ordered to "require the house of representatives, in his majesty's name, to rescind the resolution which gave birth to the circular letter," and formally as a body denounce "that rash and hasty proceeding." And if they refused? "It is the King's pleasure," Hillsborough told Bernard, "that you should immediately dissolve them."[16]

On June 30, 1768, the Massachusetts House of Representatives met to consider the question of whether to rescind the Circular Letter. This would not be a typical legislative session. It was convened at eight o'clock in the morning, earlier than usual, and members had been officially advised the day before to "attend punctually."[17] The scene in the chamber was tense, and after a few preliminary matters had been dispensed with, that tension took the form of unusual security measures.

In 1766, visitors' galleries had been installed in the House chamber so the people of Massachusetts could get a front-row view of their elected representatives in action. These were among the first public galleries ever to be installed in a legislative chamber anywhere in the world.[18] But on this day, the members of the House were taking no chances—the galleries were ordered to be cleared. In addition, the doorkeeper was ordered not to let anyone in or out of the House chamber during this debate.[19]

In this cloistered setting, the men of the Massachusetts legislature took up the question of whether or not to comply with the demand of the King and his ministers, relayed by his governor, that they rescind the resolution approving the Circular Letter. The final vote was decisive: by a margin of 92 to 17, the House voted to stand firm. In the official roll call, the first four names listed in the "Nay" column were those of James Otis, Speaker Thomas Cushing, Samuel Adams, and John Hancock.[20]

The House then drew up a lengthy letter to Governor Bernard explaining their reasoning. Another letter would be sent to Lord Hillsborough. In the letter to Bernard, the legislators pointed out that they had been willing to work with the governor "so far as could consist with the important Purposes of preserving Life, Liberty, and Property," but had been most disappointed with his conduct during this affair. In the end, they justified their actions as "actuated by a conscientious, and finally, a clear and determined Sense of Duty to God, to our King, our Country, and to our latest Posterity."[21]

A group of five House members was assembled to bring this response to Governor Bernard. He received it, and he was prepared to carry out his orders from London. The next day, July 1, the governor officially dissolved the Massachusetts legislature, leaving the colony, as Mark Puls points out, "without a democratic form of government."[22] Samuel Adams spat that this was "despotism."[23]

But the despot's victory was not exactly decisive.

Tucked into their list of reasons for refusing to back down on the Circular Letter was this very practical item: The letters had already gone out, and it would be impossible to simply pretend they had never existed. "The Circular Letters have been sent," they explained, "and many of them have been answered . . . the Public, the World must and will judge of the Proposals, Purposes and Answers."[24]

It was true that the letters had already gone out to the other colonial legislatures. The fight against the Townshend Acts was spreading beyond Massachusetts. In a few months, its next skirmish would erupt in the South, and give a brand-new politician his baptism in the fires of revolution.

WILLIAMSBURG, VIRGINIA
1769

Monday, May 8, 1769, was a busy day in Williamsburg. Of course, the opening day of the General Assembly session was always busy. This was the day when the members of the House of Burgesses, elected the previous fall, returned to the colonial capital to take their seats and begin their dealings with the royal governor—Norborne Berkeley, Baron de Botetourt, facing his first assembly as governor—and the royally appointed governor's council.

There was always a certain sense of excitement when the legislators returned. More customers came in and out of the shops and tradesmen's yards. Foot, horse, and wagon traffic picked up all along the main thoroughfare of Duke of Gloucester Street. Pubs like the popular Raleigh Tavern became unofficial hubs of political influence almost as important as the capitol building itself.

Some of the men making their way to the *official* capitol—a simple two-story brick building with a prominent porch over the main entrance on its western wall—were veteran legislators. Others were new to the House of Burgesses. Among the newcomers was one young man who would have stood out from his colleagues for any number of reasons. Perhaps it was his above-average height one noticed first—he was six feet two inches tall, some six inches taller than a typical man of his era.[25] Or perhaps it was the red hair that stuck out most to the people of Williamsburg as they noticed him in their midst.

Of course, some of them would probably have recognized Thomas Jefferson. Though he was new to the legislature, he was very familiar with Williamsburg, having studied there at the College of William & Mary just a few years earlier. Now the proud alumnus had returned to take his seat representing Albemarle County in the House of Burgesses.

The elections in the colony had taken place on November 26, 1768. Historian Jon Meacham notes that Jefferson's "campaign consisted largely of buying drinks and cakes for the landowners" who could vote.[26] The Virginia election of 1768 seems to have been a lively affair. The edition of the *Virginia Gazette* of December 15 of that year, which announced the election of "Messrs. Thomas Walker and Thomas Jefferson, for Albemarle," also reported: "At the election in New Kent, a man who had drank a little too freely, and rode a young and skittish horse, in attempting to mount, received two kicks, which in a few hours put an end to his life. We have heard of one or two more deaths at the different elections."[27]

Interestingly, the election report in this issue of the *Gazette* was relegated to page two. The front page was devoted to news from Britain and other prominent colonial capitals. Among the news from Boston, it notes: "The Earl of Hillsborough had received the letter addressed to him by the late House of Representatives in June last, relating to the circular letter of the former House to the other colonies."[28] The Massachusetts Circular Letter was still very much in the news despite the dissolution of the assembly, and as young Jefferson would soon realize, its effects were still being felt in Virginia.

At about ten that morning, Jefferson assembled with his fellow Burgesses in their chamber to take the oath of office. Eight commissioners specially appointed by the governor marched in and, assisted by the House's clerk, George Wythe, they administered the oaths. Thomas Jefferson's career in public life had officially begun. He was just a few weeks past his twenty-sixth birthday.

There followed an elaborate ritual to open the session. It involved a brief initial meeting with Governor Botetourt and the election of a Speaker—subject to the governor's approval, of course. Peyton Randolph, who had held the office previously, was elected and approved.

Then came a "very affectionate Speech" by Governor Botetourt in which he expressed his eagerness to work together with the Burgesses to "follow exactly, without Passion or Prejudice, the real Interests of those you have the Honour to represent."[29] Botetourt was generally well liked by the Virginians. One historian notes that he was "charming, generous, and diligent in attending to business," and being the first Virginia governor in decades to actually live in the colony, he "became immensely popular" after his arrival in October 1768.[30]

It was not long, however, before the governor's relations with the colonists' elected representatives would be sorely tested. Indeed, the trouble began in a matter of minutes.

When the Burgesses returned to their chamber after listening to the governor's speech, young Mr. Jefferson found himself with the first assignment of his political career. He was placed on the committee tasked with writing the Burgesses' official response to the governor's speech (a mostly routine, formal gesture). After that was dispensed with, Speaker Randolph made his first important announcement of the session.

He informed his colleagues that after the last session of the assembly, when the Massachusetts Circular Letter had been received and discussed, he had written his own letters to the other colonial legislatures expressing the Virginians' support for Massachusetts's efforts against the "sundry Acts of the British Parliament." In the intervening months, "several Letters in Answer thereto" had arrived, and Randolph submitted these "to be perused by the Members of the House."[31] The Virginia legislative session had barely begun, and already the Massachusetts controversy was being discussed.

After this announcement from Randolph, the Burgesses went about the more mundane business of organizing themselves into committees. Jefferson was assigned to two: the Committee on Privileges and Elections and the Committee on Propositions and Grievances, both of which also included, among others, George Washington and Richard Henry Lee. For the next several days, the normal business of the legislature continued apace, as the Burgesses dealt with mainly local issues.

But on May 15, there was a shift in the agenda. In a change from dealing with local matters, the Burgesses decided that on the following day they would "consider the present State of the Colony" as a whole. They specifically made sure to bring the correspondence between Speaker Randolph and the other colonial legislatures on the Massachusetts matter into the discussion.

At eleven the following morning, Thomas Jefferson took his seat as usual. He was starting to get used to the rhythm of legislative business. The morning was taken up by a number of routine matters, but later in the day that rhythm shifted palpably as the House "resolved itself into a Committee of the whole House" to discuss the broader issues facing Virginia. This was no doubt an attempt to intimidate colonial "radicals" after the controversy in Massachusetts.

The Burgesses debated these issues among themselves as a "committee of the whole." Two critical aspects of their rights as British subjects were under threat: their right to fair taxes enacted by their own representatives and the right to fair trial conducted by their own courts. After much discussion, they arrived at four resolutions, which were read out by Clerk George Wythe.

"Resolved," Wythe intoned, "that it is the opinion of this committee, that the sole right of imposing taxes on the inhabitants of this his Majesty's colony and dominion of Virginia, is now, and ever hath been legally and constitutionally vested in the House of Burgesses lawfully convened."[32]

Announcing the second resolution, Wythe declared that "it is

the undoubted privilege of the inhabitants of this colony, to petition their sovereign for redress of grievances; and that it is lawful
and expedient, to procure the concurrence of his Majesty's other
colonies."[33] The colonists had a right to not only press their case
before the King but also present a united front in doing so. This
was exactly what London feared.

The third resolution touched on the treason trial policy, with
Wythe affirming that "trials for treason . . . or for any felony or
crime whatsoever, committed and done in this his Majesty's said
colony and dominion . . . ought of right, to be had and conducted
in and before his Majesty's courts, held within the said colony."[34]
The colonists had every intention of upholding the law, but they
were equally determined to police themselves in doing so through
the lawfully constituted courts in their own colonies rather
than in England, where a fair trial would be far more difficult to
secure.

Finally, Wythe proclaimed the House's intention "that an
humble, dutiful and loyal Address be presented to his Majesty, to
assure him of our inviolable Attachment to his sacred Person and
Government," but also to ask that he "quiet the minds of his loyal
Subjects of this Colony, and to avert from them those Dangers and
Miseries" which would come from the threat of a trial across the
ocean.[35]

Thomas Jefferson joined his colleagues in adopting these resolutions unanimously. Years later, he would recall that the day was
infused with "a spirit manifestly displayed of considering the cause
of Massachusetts as a common one."[36] In keeping with that spirit
of intercolonial unity, on the rise following the Massachusetts

Circular Letter, the House also ordered copies of their resolutions to be sent "without delay" to the legislative bodies of their sister colonies.

The next day, May 17, 1769, the Burgesses picked up the business of their resolutions from the day before. They immediately ordered them printed in the *Virginia Gazette*. As it turned out, this was a wise move, and it was made none too soon. Several of the Burgesses spent the morning working on the "humble, dutiful and loyal address" to be sent to the King—and it *was* exceedingly deferential—but even that wouldn't save them. Around noon that day, Governor Botetourt struck.[37]

The Burgesses received a message that "the Governor commands the immediate attention of your House," and Speaker Randolph, George Washington, Richard Henry Lee, Thomas Jefferson, and all their colleagues left their seats to make their way to His Excellency. One account says that Botetourt was "dressed in scarlet" when he received them—perhaps adopting a more warlike posture.[38] His message was simple.

"Mr. Speaker, and Gentlemen of the House of Burgesses," he began, unfailingly polite until the end. "I have heard of your resolves, and augur ill of their effect. You have made it my duty to dissolve you, and you are dissolved accordingly." Just like that, the session was over, and the people's elected representative body in Virginia ceased to exist.

Or did it?

The House of Burgesses may have been officially dissolved, but they couldn't stop the former members from decamping from the capitol building to the Raleigh Tavern, a short distance

WEAKENING THE PEOPLE'S REPRESENTATIVES

away. There, in the privacy of the Apollo Room, they organized themselves into a "voluntary convention," as Jefferson called it.[39] Peyton Randolph, no longer holding the official title of Speaker, was elected moderator. George Washington's diary from the time records that the meeting at the tavern went on late into the night—he didn't leave until ten.[40]

The group reconvened at the Raleigh again at ten the next morning. The final outcome of their discussion was the Virginia Nonimportation Resolutions, in which the former Burgesses agreed, "by their own Example, as all other legal Ways and Means in their Power, to promote and encourage Industry and Frugality, and discourage all Manner of Luxury and Extravagance" in order to avoid purchase of any British goods that fell under the Townshend Acts, and they added a long list of other European products for good measure.[41] Eighty-eight of these "late representatives of the people," including Thomas Jefferson, then affixed their signatures to the document.

Once again, King George's royal governor had stamped out an elected legislature for placing the will of the people above the desires of the King. And just like those in Massachusetts, the Virginians refused to let that stop them. They had their resolves printed up and sent copies to the other colonies to keep the cause afloat. And when they were barred from the capitol building, there was always the tavern.

———

The stories shared here were not the only instances of the dissolution of colonial assemblies in America on the orders of royal officials. But these examples, and their common thread of the members' refusal to back down, even in the face of severe intimidation, from their duties as elected legislators shows the commitment to representative government that has undergirded our American system since even before the nation came into being. And it reminds us that the legacy of those colonial legislatures— our independent Congress and our individual state legislatures—is something precious that must be preserved.

When a royal governor moved against a legislature in the King's name, it was the ultimate act of executive coercion against the people's elected representatives. Indeed, the notion of the executive having approval of the Speaker of the legislature meant that even when harmony reigned between all parties, the legislature would never be truly independent.

In the modern United States, it is absurd to imagine so blatant an act as a president forcibly dissolving Congress, or the federal government dissolving a state legislature. But this is a direct result of Jefferson's attacking King George for his coercion of colonial assemblies—something Jefferson had experienced firsthand. Because this grievance led to the War of Independence, when the Constitution was being drafted there was special care taken to ensure that the national legislative body would be a coequal branch of government and maintain its independence from the executive. It is also why the Bill of Rights was wrapped up with the Tenth Amendment to the Constitution, which left all powers not delegated to the federal government in the hands of the state governments (primarily to be exercised by the people of the states through their state legislatures).

King George's government did not attack only the elected

colonial legislatures. The people's right to a fair trial came under attack as well, and no less a founding personage than John Hancock found himself in the King's crosshairs. The colonists' legislatures and justice system were both collapsing under the tyranny of the Crown.

CHAPTER THREE

John Adams Instructs the Crown in Its Own Law

For Depriving us in many cases, of the benefits of
Trial by Jury . . .

BOSTON HARBOR
June 10, 1768

T HE SAILORS OF THE ROYAL NAVY ATTENDED TO THEIR TASK
with grim efficiency. They boarded the trading sloop and formally took possession of her cargo in the name of His Majesty, the King. The vessel itself was to be taken in tow and impounded, to be kept under the dull gaze of Royal Navy cannons. The ship's name, in one of history's great ironies, was the *Liberty*. Its owner was a Boston merchant named John Hancock, and he was suspected of violating royal trade regulations.

The seizure of the *Liberty* provoked an outrage that whipped Boston into a frenzy—in a way that would not be seen again until the Boston Massacre, two years later. It started with the business community, as local merchants friendly to Hancock, organized by Captain Daniel Malcolm, gathered at the pier where the *Liberty* was under guard and demanded that the officials return the ship and its cargo to the rightful owner. When naval personnel ignored him, the mob of merchants turned into a riot, smashing the windows of the royal tax collectors' houses and burning one of their personal boats. Two of the tax agents were engulfed by the riot and beaten by the protesters.[1]

The British customs commissioners feared they would suffer the same fate as the collectors, so British troops were deployed to Boston for their protection. A local newspaper reported:

> At about 1 o'clock, all the troops landed under cover of the cannon of the ships of war, and marched into the Common, with muskets charged, bayonets fixed, colours flying, drums beating and fifes, &c. playing, making with the train of artillery upwards of 700 men.[2]

This occupation only angered Bostonians further, as the troops outside their houses came to represent the King's increasing authority and intrusion into their daily lives. This incident was more than a dispute over smuggling. When the matter finally came to court some months later, this was exactly the argument that Hancock's attorney—his friend John Adams—would make. The popular outrage at the *Liberty*'s seizure gave Adams the fuel he needed to hold a fire to British legal authority.

COURT OF VICE ADMIRALTY, MASSACHUSETTS BAY COLONY
Winter 1769

When John Adams entered the courtroom of Judge Robert Auchmuty, he could not have helped but feel slightly out of his depth.

He was, of course, a talented attorney, but revenue litigation was still a new field for him, and the British admiralty court was a proving ground for his abilities.

The admiralty courts as employed under King George were a dramatic break from British legal tradition. The courts consisted of judges appointed by the King and were often populated by those sympathetic to the interests of the Crown. Prior to the Sugar Act of 1763, these types of courts were used primarily to settle commercial disputes concerning trade.[3]

Across the room stood Jonathan Sewall, who was serving as the attorney for the Crown. Sewall was advocate general of the Massachusetts Bay Colony and a veteran lawyer for the King. In prosecuting John Hancock, Sewall demanded he pay penalties amounting to the extraordinary sum of £9,000.[4]

Despite facing off against each other in this courtroom, Adams and Sewall shared a complicated relationship as friend and foe. Though their profession brought them into adversarial contact, the two maintained a close and jovial friendship outside of their trials. Just prior to the case, Sewall had personally offered Adams the chance to take his position as advocate general. Adams declined this honor repeatedly, telling his friend that accepting the position to work on behalf of Parliament and the Crown would be "wholly inconsistent with all my ideas of right, justice, and policy."[5]

Had Adams accepted Sewall's offer, he would not only have been standing on that opposite side of the courtroom, arguing in defense of the King's authority, but he also would have been handsomely rewarded if successful. That was the prospect that awaited Sewall. For bringing the charges on behalf of the King, Sewall would have been entitled to one-third of the damages a defendant found guilty would pay.

But Adams was fighting for something more than financial spoils. The defendant in this case was his friend and fellow patriot John Hancock. Of course, that meant Adams was under added pressure to prevail. This was more than just a dispute over taxes—his friend's honor was at stake. And importantly, this case was a chance for Adams to take a stand against the decidedly unfair trend in the King's idea of justice.

British officials undermined the tradition of English common law when they sought to expand the powers of the juryless courts to unilaterally enforce their statutes. Generally speaking, until the 1760s, the American colonies' relations with the mother country were in an unofficial state of "salutary neglect," in which royal officials chose to only loosely enforce regulations over the American colonies. Therefore, criminal trade cases, such as avoiding duties on imports, were rarely upheld against traders like John Hancock. During this period, American colonists developed a feeling of general autonomy and liberty as a society operating far away from the Crown.

But this policy of "salutary neglect" was rolled back under King George III and was all but shattered with the Sugar Act of 1764. Under this law, the admiralty courts were granted the ability to rule on violations of customs and smuggling laws, meaning that British officials could direct cases to friendly judges when they felt that courts using local juries would rule against their interests.[6] Judges friendly to the King could then unilaterally convict without a jury, in many cases turning the courts into a political tool to deprive the colonists of their freedoms. This meant that John Hancock was being tried under a law in whose passage he had had no say and without a jury of his peers—violating his rights as a British subject.

————

Settling in at his desk before the judge's bench, Adams carefully pored over the notes he had made for his argument. Hancock had been charged with failing to pay the full duty to the British Crown before his crew unloaded his cargo of Portuguese Madeira, a type of fortified wine. Royal officials claimed that Hancock had even boasted of his plans to defy the authority of these taxes.

His ship had arrived in Boston on the night of May 9, 1768. On the tenth, the crew reportedly unloaded twenty-five "Pipes" of wine, which were duly logged and taxed by the customs official. But another customs officer later emerged with a story that he had been forcibly locked in the hold by the *Liberty*'s crew—Hancock's employees—on the night of the ninth while they illegally unloaded a great deal of wine before their "official" unloading on the tenth.[7]

All told, the Crown accused Hancock of unloading one hundred pipes of wine in the dead of night to avoid paying the King's taxes. And this was no small amount—each pipe contained about 126 gallons.[8] Madeira was, to say the least, a very popular libation in colonial America.

The British prosecutors lacked sufficient evidence to fully prove that Hancock had taken part in smuggling, but Adams still faced an uphill struggle. He understood the difficulty of arguing before a judge who was friendly to the King, especially when the opposing evidence consisted of testimony from British duty collectors and other royal officials.[9] With this in mind, he decided against focusing strictly on the issue of revenue. He decided he would make a legal argument that would change the course of history in the colonies.

Meanwhile, his opposing counsel, Jonathan Sewall, was concluding his remarks before the court, stating:

> John Hancock . . . well knowing, that the Duties thereon were not paid or secured and that the unshipping and landing the same, as aforesaid, was with Intent to defraud the said Lord the King as aforesaid, and contrary to Law.[10]

Adams silently gave thanks to Providence for giving him the wisdom not to take Sewall's job. He knew he could not bear to stand as a royal advocate in a court that was—at least in this case—less a chamber of fair legal proceedings and more a political tool of King George III. One grievance in particular would become the crux of Adams's argument: Missing from that admiralty courtroom was a jury of Hancock's peers.

Under English law, cases such as smuggling were typically tried as a criminal offense in a court with a judge and a jury of citizens. The tradition of assembling a jury of peers to determine a citizen's guilt dated back to 1215 and the foundational document of English law, the Magna Carta. This seminal charter established the idea of judgment by one's peers as a foundation of a free society. Clause 39 states: "No man shall be taken, outlawed, banished, or in any way destroyed, nor will we proceed against or prosecute him, except by the lawful judgment of his peers and by the law of the land."[11] Guilt was to be decided not by one man but rather by a group of his peers, naturally employing the norms and standards embraced by their society. But apparently things could change if a monarch decided to tighten his grip on his far-off colonies, as King George III did in the 1760s.

Thus, by the time the court proceedings began in November 1768, *Jonathan Sewall v. John Hancock* had taken on a greater significance than simply proving Hancock's innocence; it was a challenge to the tyrannical foundations of the very court in which they stood. John Adams was aware of this and, brilliant legal mind that he was, crafted his argument accordingly. He wanted to win the case to help his comrade as well as to send a message.

His opposition tried to wear him down with procedural sandbagging. Judge Auchmuty prolonged the trial with countless excessive witness testimonies. Adams described it in his autobiography as "a painfull Drudgery," claiming there were few days without a court hearing during the winter of 1768–69.[12] But the drawn-out trial, covered extensively by patriot broadsheets, combined with the presence of British Regulars in the city, kept patriot anger alive in Boston for the entire duration of the case.

In his ultimate defense, John Adams invoked both English common law and the Magna Carta to challenge the legitimacy of juryless criminal courts. His condemnation of the admiralty courts quickly gained traction in the public square.[13] His argument that Hancock could not be convicted for smuggling hinged on several points.

On the practical side he argued that, because it was Hancock's crew who had allegedly committed this act, the government could not prove that Hancock himself had any awareness of the alleged wrongdoing. "Can it be proved that Mr. Hancock knew of this Frolick?" Adams asked. "If he neither consented to it, nor knew of it, how can he be liable to the penalty?"[14]

But his more powerful arguments attacked the grounding of the law under which Hancock was being tried, and the court in which the case was brought. Adams argued that because American colonists lacked representation in Parliament, Hancock was being unjustly tried under a law in the passage of which he had had no say. "My client Mr. Hancock never consented to it," Adams declared. "He never voted for it himself, and he never voted for any man to make such a law for him. In this respect therefore the greatest consolation of an Englishman, suffering under any Law, is torn from him, I mean the Reflection, that it is a Law of his own Making."[15]

Building upon this, Adams then proceeded to make another, ultimately stronger, argument that the Crown had infringed upon Hancock's fundamental rights as an English subject. In so doing, he invoked the original underpinnings of the English judicial system and sought to prove that the King had exceeded his authority under the law. By giving power to the admiralty court to hold trials without juries, Adams argued, the Crown violated the Magna Carta.

Excoriating the misuse of admiralty courts, he reasoned that "these extraordinary penalties and forfeitures, are to be heard and tried—how? Not by a jury, not by the law of the land—by the civil law and a single judge." He argued that in a betrayal of the noble English barons who wrote (and forced King John to sign) the original Magna Carta, "the Barons of modern times have answered that they are willing, that the Laws of England should be changed, at least with Regard to all America." This persecution of Hancock was less than what an English subject deserved. "Here is the Contrast that stares us in the Face!" He announced:

> The Parliament in one clause guarding the people of the realm, and securing to them the Benefit of a trial by the law of the land, and by the next clause, depriving all Americans of that privilege. What shall we say to this Distinction? Is there not in this Clause, a Brand of Infamy, of Degradation, and Disgrace, fixed upon every American? Is he not degraded below the Rank of an Englishman? Is it not directly, a Repeal of Magna Charta, as far as America is concerned?[16]

This argument proved successful, and it led to a public victory for the growing patriot movement. On March 25, 1796, Jonathan Sewall withdrew the case. Adams had defeated his close friend in court. But he had done much more than that.

Sewall v. Hancock expanded the legal foundations for American independence and the colonists' case for claiming the fundamental right to a fair and independent judicial system. King George III had used the Trade and Navigation Acts to consolidate power over the colonies' judicial systems. King George's expansion of admiralty courts showed the colonists that a free and independent court system—one that sought to uphold the fundamental and original values of a free, law-abiding society—was something worth fighting for. In the Declaration of Independence, Jefferson made sure to accuse King George of "depriving us in many cases, of the benefits of Trial by Jury."

It is therefore easy to understand that, when the American revolutionaries became Founders, they felt so strongly about the need to disperse power among the three coequal branches of government and prohibit any one branch from unduly influencing another. After the Constitution had been drafted but prior to its ratification, James Madison warned the nation in Federalist paper 48: "The powers properly belonging to one of the departments ought not to be directly and completely administered by either of the other departments. It is equally evident, that none of them ought to possess, directly or indirectly, an overruling influence over the others."[17]

This included keeping the judiciary independent and preventing its use as a tool of coercion, as the British admiralty courts had become in the American colonies prior to the Revolution. King George had used the power to exercise justice in his name to destroy a fundamental right outlined in the Magna Carta, which the King himself was supposed to enforce. He and his government violated the foundational limits that were placed upon him by the people, and the Founders sought to prevent that from ever occurring again.

John Adams used that argument to turn the Hancock case into a prominent public victory for the growing patriot movement in Massachusetts. But for his fellow colonists in North Carolina, however, who were trying to set up their own court system, justice was proving more elusive.

CHAPTER FOUR

Centralizing Power

He has refused his Assent to Laws, the most wholesome and necessary for the public good.

He has obstructed the Administration of Justice, by refusing his Assent to Laws for establishing Judiciary powers.

He has made Judges dependent on his Will alone, for the tenure of their offices, and the amount and payment of their salaries.

NEW BERN, NORTH CAROLINA
February 1773

A COLD WINTER WIND CAME OFF THE ATLANTIC OCEAN, CUT-ting through the night and blowing west, sending waves crashing onto the beaches of North Carolina's Outer Banks and winding its way up the Neuse River to the town of New Bern. There its ferocity soon ran up against the most imposing structure in town: the Governor's Palace, where candles could be seen still burning in the upper floor of the main house despite the late hour.

Inside, an even greater storm was brewing inside the mind of Governor Josiah Martin. He had hoped to have a quiet job ruling over a quiet backwater colony. He was wrong. By the time he first arrived in North Carolina, he found that tensions had been brewing for some time.

The revolutionary fervor that swept through many of Britain's North American colonies in the late 1760s had not passed North Carolina by. In 1769, Speaker of the House John Harvey had laid before the assembly "a letter which he received from the Speaker of the House of Burgesses in Virginia inclosing sundry resolutions of that House."[1]

These were the resolutions passed in Virginia on May 16, 1769, which asserted that Britain's North American colonists had the right to tax themselves, petition the King for redress of grievances, and receive a fair trial—as well as a fourth resolution, determining that an appeal be made to the King directly to address these issues. In Virginia, the governor had dissolved the House of Burgesses the day after they passed these resolutions (but not before they were printed up and copies sent "to the Speakers of the several Houses of Assembly, on this continent"[2]). In North Carolina, then governor Tryon waited four days before doing the same. The same John Harvey who had introduced these resolutions remained the Speaker of the House in the current session, and now he was Governor Martin's problem.

But North Carolina's issues were not confined to the legislature. Far from New Bern, in the western interior—the "backcountry"— independent-minded settlers had long bristled against the taxes and rules that the royal government based in the east had tried to impose on them. These hardy backcountrymen were known as the "Regulators," and sometimes their resistance turned violent.

In 1770–71, Regulators assaulted local officials and even confronted Governor Tryon and the colonial militia. The Regulator hostilities culminated in the Battle of Alamance in 1771, in which the rebellion was effectively put down by the government, which immediately began issuing pardons to Regulators in hopes of defusing the situation.[3]

Though Governor Martin had not faced the violence of the Regulators the way his predecessor had, the tensions remained. A major source of contention was the colony's court system, which had been on shaky ground for several years.

The judicial system in North Carolina had been "unsettled, changeable and uncertain" for some time, well before Governor Martin took office, and even before George III took the throne of Great Britain. In April 1754, the government of George III's grandfather King George II—George III's father had died young, before taking the throne, so the crown passed from grandfather to grandson—raised an objection to a law passed in North Carolina eight years prior, in 1746. This statute set up courts for the colony, but the British government felt that setting up courts was something that only the King's government could do directly. It could not be done by the people of the colony themselves. Accordingly, they "disallowed" the 1746 law, effectively shutting down North Carolina's courts.[4]

The fact that the British government saw fit to act retroactively against a law passed eight years prior was yet another failure of their colonial policy. They failed to understand—or were simply unconcerned by—the notion that vast gaps in time and location between the people controlling the laws and the people affected by those laws do not make for a smooth-running government. A sudden change in what appeared to be settled law would seem extremely arbitrary to the people of North Carolina who were familiar with the prior system. The settled expectations of the people—the rules of the game—had been upended, and this does not create the conditions for good governance.

Perhaps anticipating this, the government's man on the ground in North Carolina, Governor Arthur Dobbs, acted quickly to remedy the situation, and in January 1755 he approved new laws to set up colonial courts, which solved the problem until April 1759, when George II's government once again took issue with North Carolina's judicial system.[5] While London's position had softened since 1754—it no longer objected to the North Carolinians setting up their own courts altogether—it still felt the laws gave too much power to the local judicial authorities at the expense of the King.[6] The local county judges were, after all, more attuned to the sense of justice of the people who would be appearing before their benches, but to London it was the King's justice, not the people's, that mattered most.

In 1760, the colonists tried again, and in May of that year Governor Dobbs approved a law that once again established courts in North Carolina but added a Suspension Clause, which according to historian Edward Dumbauld rendered the law "temporary for two years until the King's pleasure could be known."[7] Given the finicky nature of the "King's pleasure" when it came to North Carolina's court laws, the inclusion of this provision was understandable from the governor's perspective. The "King's pleasure" was made known in December 1761, and by this time, there was a new king: George III. His government followed that of his predecessor by once again striking down the law and even admonished Governor Dobbs for daring to approve it.[8] But Governor Dobbs's luck turned in 1762, when he was able to oversee a compromise court bill crafted between the upper and lower houses of the North Carolina legislature and which also drew no ire from the government in London.[9] For the moment, there was a place for justice in North Carolina again—the King's justice, at least.

The problem that would become Governor Martin's began in January 1768, when his predecessor, William Tryon, approved the renewal of the court laws. They contained a provision known as an Attachment Clause—a means by which North Carolinians could seek repayment of debts owed to them by people who did not live in the colony by "attaching," or garnishing, the property of their debtors.[10] It gave the people of North Carolina some legal protections against absent British landowners, merchants, or anyone else who did business in the colony from afar and didn't pay their debts.

There were no issues with this provision until 1770, when an eagle-eyed adviser to the British Board of Trade happened upon it and raised the alarm.[11] Historian Herbert Friedenwald recounts that the British government, upon review, found the Attachment Clause to be "a serious departure from legal form," but was magnanimous enough not to simply scrap the entire law as they'd done in the past. Instead, they merely suggested that the North Carolina Assembly amend the law to remove the problematic language on attachments. When this had not happened by February 1772, King George III formally instructed the new governor to refuse to approve any new court laws with an Attachment Clause unless they also contained a Suspension Clause—essentially making the law temporary and subject to the King's approval.[12]

The governor to whom this edict was given was Josiah Martin, in whose hands the problem of North Carolinian justice currently rested. The court laws of 1768 were due to expire in 1773, and now the session had commenced in which they had to be renewed if courts were to remain in operation in the colony.

This was not the only example of the royal government interfering in the judicial affairs of the colonies. When the people of South Carolina, for instance, attempted in 1768 to set up more courts so that everyone was not required to travel to Charleston for justice, the King struck down the law—only because it provided that judges be paid "contingent upon their appointment during good behavior instead of during the king's pleasure."[13] The Pennsylvanians, too, suffered "an entire failure in the administration of justice in this province" when Queen Anne's government struck down their court law in 1706. Courts were reestablished but struck down again in 1714, only to be set up once more.[14]

Still, the North Carolina court controversy was a protracted dispute between colonists and the royal government that would, under the somewhat hapless Governor Martin, grow into a full-blown crisis. Over its course, the royal government would attack not only the judicial but the legislative representation of the North

Carolina colonists—and the end to the crisis would come only in full-blown revolution.

———————

As he sat brooding in his New Bern office, winds beating on his windows, Martin was in the midst of what was shaping up to be an extremely contentious session of the North Carolina legislature. It was hardly a surprise that the trouble was coming from the legislature's lower house, formally known as the House of Commons—borrowing the term from the "Mother of Parliaments" in London—but commonly called the assembly. The members of this body were elected by the colonists. It was up to the upper house—His Majesty's Honorable Council, whose members were appointed by royal decree—as well as Governor Martin himself to rein in the popular passions of the assembly and make sure business went smoothly in this corner of King George III's empire.

At the moment, Governor Martin knew things were not going very smoothly at all, and he had a feeling they were about to get worse. He paced nervously up and down his study, sometimes sitting down at his desk, where pen and paper were arrayed, along with copies of the notes from the assembly session so far. But he never sat long before he resumed his pacing, running his hand absentmindedly along the elegantly carved chairs and tables in the room or fingering the hand-tooled leather bindings of the many books in his library.

He was struggling to write a letter to William Legge, the second Earl of Dartmouth, in London. Lord Dartmouth was serving as secretary of state for the colonies, King George's right-hand man when it came to managing the affairs of Britain's far-flung possessions. Lord Dartmouth was the middleman between the King and his colonial governors, and Martin knew that when His Lordship sent a message, it may have been written in his handwriting, but it spoke with the King's voice. At the same time, Martin knew whatever he wrote to Lord Dartmouth would be passed directly to the King, along with Dartmouth's opinion on how Martin was handling himself across the ocean. To hold the favor of Lord Dartmouth, therefore, was to hold the favor of the King himself.

Governor Martin went back to his desk again, determined to choose his words carefully. He had hoped to send word back to London once the assembly had accomplished something positive, but he saw a fight brewing and felt it was his duty to warn Lord Dartmouth. But how? It was critical that he show his superiors that he had the matter in hand. At thirty-five, he was facing the biggest challenge of his career—a career that had so far been unimpressive. The army hadn't quite worked out. But he had been given a chance at a new start when he was appointed governor of North Carolina in 1771. Now, deep down, in thoughts that came to him only late at night, when he was the only one awake in the Governor's Palace, he was wondering if he was truly up to the task.

Josiah Martin's family originally came from Ireland, and he was born in Dublin, but the Martins were decidedly a colonial family. The family, according to historian Vernon Stumpf, "belonged to the country gentry class that had helped staff British imperial and provincial agencies since the sixteenth century." Martin's family was based at Antigua in the West Indies, and he had an uncle, also named Josiah Martin, living on Long Island,

New York. Josiah the nephew would marry the daughter of Josiah the uncle—his first cousin. Thanks to "marriage alliances and careful investment," Stumpf notes, the Martins "acquired estates and plantations in the British Isles, the islands of the Caribbean, and North America."[15]

They also sought to acquire positions of influence for themselves. Young Josiah's first attempt at this had been to enter the British Army, where he served as an officer from 1756 to 1769. Despite this lengthy service, during which he eventually reached the rank of lieutenant colonel, army life did not seem to agree with Martin. Finding himself in failing health and short on money, he sold off his military commission in 1769.[16] In need of a new occupation, he sought the aid of his older half brother Samuel Martin, a well-connected Member of Parliament who held influence not only in politics but in royal circles as well, thanks to his service as treasurer to Princess Augusta, the King's mother.[17]

Samuel was close with Lord Hillsborough, who was then serving as secretary of state for the colonies. When North Carolina's governor, William Tryon, was sent north to become governor of New York, Samuel's influence helped get Josiah Martin named to fill the vacancy.[18] Josiah was not totally unqualified for the position—thanks to his uncle's influence, he had been able to dabble somewhat in the colonial administration in New York.[19] But his debut as a royal governor did not have an auspicious beginning. His health problems flared up again—this time requiring multiple operations—and he was prevented from making the trip to North Carolina for some time.[20]

But now, as he sat at his desk not quite two years later, Josiah Martin was very much in charge—on paper, at least. It was his responsibility to keep a firm hand on the troublemakers in the North Carolina Assembly, a task that was proving difficult.

Tensions between the colonists and the government had been rising for some time. As he looked around his sumptuously appointed office in the Governor's Palace, he was reminded once again, with a sinking feeling, that the ungrateful colonists even begrudged him these grand surroundings in the midst of which he sat.

The brick palace had been the brainchild of Governor Tryon— or more specifically, that of John Hawks, the architect whom Tryon had brought over from England specifically to build a new colonial administration building and governor's residence for North Carolina. Tryon formalized New Bern as the colony's capital and sought to erect the capitol building as an unassailable symbol of British elegance and power. Hawks drew up plans in the up-to-the-minute Georgian style, a grand brick main house with curved, colonnaded wings coming out from both sides, each of which was anchored with a smaller brick structure at the end.[21] Construction began in 1767 and finished in 1770, when the building was formally opened with great ceremony and the Tryon family moved in.[22]

Less inclined to celebrate were the average North Carolina colonists, particularly in the backcountry. In 1766 the assembly had initially appropriated five thousand pounds for the project, and to do so, they dipped into an existing fund for public construction—specifically, it would otherwise have been used to build schools. In 1768, it was determined that the ongoing construction would cost an additional ten thousand pounds, which was promptly appropriated from the public coffers. To compensate for this expense, the government did what governments are notorious for doing when they go over budget—they increased taxes. North Carolinians were subjected to liquor taxes and a poll tax, and they were none too pleased.[23] The citizens of Orange County, in the western part of the colony, lodged a protest in 1768, declaring: "We are determined not to pay the Tax for the next three years, for the Edifice or Governor's House. We want no such House, nor will we pay for it."[24]

But the "Edifice" remained. While Governor Tryon did not get to enjoy his creation for very long before he left for New York in 1771, Governor Martin, as the first governor to commence his term in what was deemed "the finest government house in the colonies," wasted no time in putting his own stamp on the place.[25] A later historian would note that Martin "proceeded to fill the building with lavish furnishings at a time when the seeds of revolution were being sown in North Carolina and Britain's other American colonies."[26]

These "lavish furnishings" were small comfort to Governor Martin as he sat dejected in his study, listening to the wind howl outside. As he looked out the window, he noticed how low the wicks of the candles in the candelabra on the windowsill had gotten. A glance at the clock told him it was later than he thought. He knew he had to begin his letter if he was going to get it started on its journey to London by messenger at first light. He pushed all thoughts of revolutionaries, regulators, and his own career prospects out of his mind and took up his pen.

"I have the honour to inform your Lordship," he began, and proceeded to explain to Lord Dartmouth that he had called the colonial legislature to order on January 25, "when"—he thought it might be best to open with some good news—"the House of Assembly was fuller, as I am informed, than it has ever been at the beginning of a Session."[27] He was pleased with himself for remembering to include that detail. He continued his account of the opening of the assembly: "I then entertained the fairest hopes, that such a temper would govern their deliberations, & such measures be adopted, as could not fail to distinguish the Session honorably." Martin's hopes, he explained to Lord Dartmouth, "were formed upon the information I had received, that the people had made a better choice of Representatives than usual."[28]

Good, Martin thought to himself. Lord Dartmouth must understand that he thought he would be dealing with rational legislators, a better crop than usual—that they turned out to be otherwise could hardly be seen as Martin's fault. But realizing it would probably be prudent to highlight the wisdom of the royal agenda he put before the assembly, Martin added that his high hopes for this session also rested "upon my own Assurance, that I had nothing in Command from His Majesty to propose, that could cause the least difficulty or embarrassment."[29]

Martin set down his pen and read over what he'd written so far. Certainly he had painted himself in the best possible light, but it was still the honest truth that he'd begun the assembly session with high hopes for its success.

"Gentlemen of His Majesty's Honorable Council," he had begun the formal opening proceedings on January 25 of that year (the King's representatives always came first), "Mr. Speaker, and Gentlemen of the House of Assembly." Martin remembered looking out at the assembled legislators. "I have chosen to meet you in General Assembly at this time of the year," he continued, "not only in regard to the common convenience of the members of the Legislature, but in assurance that as it is the season of most perfect leisure your minds will be entirely disengaged and disposed to enter upon the public business with all that calm fixed and deliberate attention which the momentous concerns of your Country seem now peculiarly to demand."[30] With these words he had sought to put the men of the assembly in a good mood and encourage them to behave responsibly. Little had he known then that his entreaty would fall upon deaf ears.

He then went on to describe the business before the session, beginning—he hoped strategically—with an announcement of the King's intention to pardon those colonists who had taken part in the recent Regulator fracas. He followed that, however, with a lecture on the importance of defending the colony from "offenders against the public peace."[31]

Governor Martin then came to a trickier part of the legislative agenda. Various colonial statutes were due to expire this year, and it would be the task of this session of the assembly to renew them. "The expiration of many fundamental Laws at this time," Martin reminded the members, "will furnish you with much business for the ensuing Session." He paused slightly before mentioning the most pressing of these, and the one most likely to prove contentious.

Of all the laws in need of renewal, Martin declared, "there appears to me none of greater consequence than the laws for the constitution of the Superior and Inferior Courts, the Channels by which we derive from our Sovereign that distributive Justice so essential to the security of Liberty and Prosperity, and that is so eminently the Blessing of British Subjects."[32] North Carolina's court system was in disarray, and had been for some time. With the expiration of the court laws this term, Martin had a chance to preside over and overhaul the colony's court system, and he was not about to miss the opportunity to do so.

He explained that it was "no less my desire than my duty to promote the reputation of this Colony"—and perhaps, though he did not mention it, promote his own reputation as well. To that end, he urged the legislators "to frame the Laws relating to those Institutions upon the most liberal principles of Equity to make them permanent." The colony needed a stable judicial system—but according to the King's sense of justice, of course. "By these means, Gentlemen," exhorted Martin, "you will essentially raise the credit of your Country, give dignity and stability to its Courts of Judicature and obviate those great inconveniences and disadvantages that are incident to every state whose fundamental constitutions are unsettled, changeable and uncertain."[33]

———

Up late in his office, Martin contemplated the next phase of his letter to Lord Dartmouth. He had begun with a pleasing account of the opening of the assembly, and an explanation of why he had every reason to expect it to go well. He had ably laid out a reasonable royal agenda before "a better choice of Representatives than usual." He knew he had to shift the scene, but how? He began to write:

"These favorable appearances, my Lord, lasted until the 24th, when the House of Assembly presented to me a Bill 'to Amend and continue an Act passed in the year 1768, for Establishing Superior Courts' etc., that by its limitation, would expire at the end of the present Session, which my duty obliged me to reject." Martin hastened to explain that the bill was "repugnant to His Majesty's Royal Instructions, relating to the attachment of effects of persons who have never resided in the Colony." Martin added that "this indispensable conduct of mine"—surely Lord Dartmouth would understand he was simply doing his job—spurred the members of the assembly to look into the attachment question, and the effect of the King's instructions, in more detail.[34]

Once they had done so, the rumblings were not favorable. "I was yesterday informed," Governor Martin reported, "that there was a temperate but firm resolution in the majority of the House, rather to be without Courts of Justice, than conform to the direction of that Instruction."[35] The people's elected representatives of North Carolina would rather shut down their courts than subject them to the unfair dictates of King George's justice.

As Governor Martin drew his letter to a conclusion, his heart swelled. He knew where his loyalties lay, and he wasn't about to allow these backcountry rabble-rousers to push him around. "Whatever may be the event," he wrote, "I do assure your Lordship, nothing on my part shall be wanting to bring the Session to such conclusion, as may be most conducive to the Public Welfare, and consistent with the honor of His Majesty's Government, and my Duty to my Royal Master."[36] The letter was ready to go and would be sent by messenger as soon as possible in the morning. Martin went to bed determined that North Carolina would be ruled under the King's justice or none at all.

NEW BERN, NORTH CAROLINA
March 1773

It had become apparent that the people of North Carolina preferred no justice to that of King George III. The assembly, led by its revolutionarily minded Speaker John Harvey, had refused to yield on the subject of attachments in the court bill. On March 6, Governor Martin had agreed to sign a court bill complete with the Attachment Clause but also containing a Suspension Clause, pending the King's approval—but he was well aware that that approval would never come, rendering that bill effectively toothless and leaving the colony still without a court system.[37] Still hoping to arrive at a more permanent solution, Martin then "prorogued," or suspended, the legislature for three days. North Carolina historian Milton Ready explains that this was "an effort to make the members more willing to yield on the attachments clause" and "give them time to think it over."[38]

It did not have the desired effect. Governor Martin attempted to reconvene the assembly but found that most of its members had skipped town. As Ready recounted, "Most of the representatives simply went home."[39]

Now, on March 12, Martin was struggling to find the words to report this latest setback to Lord Dartmouth in London. He did not mince words, recalling at once that his previous letter "implied my apprehensions that little public advantage would result" from this legislative session, "which I am concerned to inform your Lordships proved but too just and prophetic of the Event." He went on to explain that he had suspended the assembly until the ninth. But "on the morning of that day," he reported, "when I was preparing to open a new Session, I received information by the Clerk of the Assembly, with great surprise that there was not remaining in Town a sufficient number of Members."[40] Martin recounted that he consulted with the Council, and then he decided to dissolve the legislative session formally—though in reality all he did was make official the dissolution that had already occurred in practice.

In his study, trying to make sense of the situation, Martin realized that there was no way to explain this that made him look favorable in Lord Dartmouth's eyes. He made sure to add, therefore, that though these events "must appear to you very irregular . . . it is not altogether unprecedented in this Colony." Furthermore, he allowed that "I have the satisfaction to find, and to assure your Lordship, no ill humor or disposition, has been discovered towards me."[41] Government officials have always had a knack for finding ways to assure others "all is well" even as control slips speedily from their grasp.

After burnishing his own image, Martin then proceeded to shift blame onto the colonists' insistence on protection from non-paying debtors. "The truth is, My Lord, they wanted a concession of the Privilege of Attachment as they call it, at all events," he explained, before suggesting there was personal mercenary motivation behind it: "I have reason to think it was the more strenuously insisted upon to serve the interests of some persons who had attachments actually depending."[42] Even if that were true, collection of payments owed is supposed to be part of any functioning justice system—unless, of course, you were a North Carolina colonist and the person who owed you money was safely across the ocean.

This issue was never fully resolved for the people of North Carolina. Governor Martin attempted to set up his own courts directly under his authority, and through him the King's. But this was not acceptable to the North Carolinians, and the assembly used their "power of the purse" to shut down this scheme—they refused to appropriate funds to pay his judges.[43] There was essentially no judicial system in North Carolina from 1773 until the end of British rule, and this impasse helped bring all legislative business between the governor and the assembly to a near complete standstill.[44]

An account of the difficulties this imposed on the people of the colony is left by a distinguished visitor, the Boston patriot Josiah Quincy, who traveled on revolutionary business throughout the southern colonies in 1773. In early April he passed through North Carolina, and reported:

> The present state of North Carolina is really curious; there are but five provincial laws in force through the Colony, and no courts at all in being. No one can recover a debt, except before a single magistrate, where the sums are within his jurisdiction, and offenders escape with impunity. The people are in great consternation about the matter; what will be the consequence is problematical.[45]

The consequence was "problematical" indeed: this "great consternation" among the people—brought about by the obstinacy of the royal government—helped propel North Carolina into the revolutionary cause with such fervor that it became the first colony to formally authorize its delegates to the Continental Congress to vote for independence from Great Britain. That same Congress would memorialize the North Carolinians' fight for justice in the Declaration of Independence.

———

How did such a local issue merit its own mention in a document of national—indeed, international—importance? Herbert Friedenwald suggests North Carolina was singled out due to "the political consideration that she had been the earliest to declare in favor of independence."[46] Sydney George Fisher, another historian, notes that he was "able to find only one instance"—that of North Carolina—"in which a colony was deprived of courts by the king disallowing the law establishing them."[47] Even at the time, Thomas Hutchinson, the former royal governor of Massachusetts who decamped for England and from there wrote a scathing rebuttal to the Declaration of Independence, found this judicial grievance obscure. He found himself "somewhat at a loss, upon first reading this article, to what transaction or to what Colony it could refer," but "soon found, that the Colony must be North Carolina" and proceeded to blame the colonists instead of the King.[48] Perhaps Fisher was unaware that Hutchinson was unfamiliar with, or chose to ignore, the similar problems that had cropped up in South Carolina and Pennsylvania.

No colonial court crisis, however, was as dramatic as the situation in North Carolina, but these other accounts of the Crown's judicial malfeasance may shed some light on why, in his rough draft of the Declaration, Jefferson made clear that this court meddling had occurred in multiple places. His original version of this grievance read: "He has suffered the administration of justice totally to cease in some of these colonies, refusing his assent to laws for establishing judiciary powers."[49] Note the use of the plural in "some of these colonies."

When the Committee of Five edited Jefferson's draft, the word *colonies* was changed to *states*. Julian Boyd, editor of Jefferson's papers, points out that "states" was added in handwriting other than Jefferson's, and Boyd was "inclined to believe that it is in the handwriting of John Adams."[50]

The changes made to these lines by the whole of the Congress were more significant. They rendered the "states" versus "colonies" question irrelevant, making the statement more general and also softening it to read as follows: "He has obstructed the Administration of Justice, by refusing his Assent to Laws for establishing Judiciary Powers." But in North Carolina, at least, Jefferson's original language was closer to the truth—it had not merely been "obstructed"; it had totally ceased.

Still, the wording of the final Declaration has a greater bearing when considering the modern implications of this issue. After independence, conflicts between the judiciary and the executive (as opposed to the monarch) did not disappear. In fact, this conflict flared up again to play a central role in an especially sad episode in America's early history as a nation: the removal of the Cherokee from Georgia.

The U.S. Supreme Court ruled in *Worcester v. Georgia* in 1832 that the Cherokee nation was "a distinct community occupying its own territory in which the laws of Georgia can have no force."[51] Any dealings with Native American tribes, Chief Justice John Marshall concluded, were up to the federal government, not state governments. "The whole intercourse between the United States and this nation," his opinion explained, "is, by our constitution and laws, vested in the government of the United States."[52] This meant that the state of Georgia's repeated attempts to push the Cherokee off their land or otherwise squeeze them out by regulation—including the law they used to arrest Samuel Worcester, a missionary living among them—were illegal.

But the executive branch would have to enforce this ruling to force Georgia to back down, and President Andrew Jackson refused to do so. He is widely reported to have remarked: "John Marshall has made his decision; now let him enforce it." In reality, this quotation is a distillation of a longer statement he made to Brigadier General John Coffee: "The decision of the supreme court has fell still born, and they find that it cannot coerce Georgia to yield to its mandate."[53] The effect was the same: Jackson indicated that the court could not enforce its own decision, and he would decline to do so.

The end result, as history shows, was all too painful. Jackson not only refused to help enforce the court's ruling but also continued to support policies of forced Native American removal and even sent troops to remove the Cherokee from the land in question. The Cherokee then embarked westward on their tragic Trail of Tears. For many, perhaps even into the thousands, that journey proved fatal. All because the voice of the people's justice went unheeded.

A more modern story, with a very different ending, shows the importance of a judiciary that stands up to the executive. In 1952, while the United States was engaged in the Korean War—a "war" which began, it must be noted, without a formal congressional declaration thereof—President Harry Truman attempted to seize

America's steel mills to head off a labor dispute that, his administration felt, would hamper production critical to the war effort. In his executive order authorizing the seizure, Truman declared that "a work stoppage would immediately jeopardize and imperil our national defense and the defense of those joined with us in resisting aggression, and would add to the continuing danger of our soldiers, sailors, and airmen engaged in combat in the field."[54]

The day after Truman made his announcement at an emergency hearing, attorneys for the steel companies made a request for a restraining order to stop the president. The presiding judge—who had himself been appointed by Truman—denied their request.[55] A later court appearance led to a ruling in the steel companies' favor, and the case made its way to the Supreme Court as *Youngstown Sheet & Tube Co. v. Sawyer.* The court ruled that Truman had exceeded his authority and that his action "was not authorized by the Constitution or laws of the United States, and it cannot stand." Furthermore, there was "no statute which expressly or impliedly authorizes the President to take possession of this property as he did."[56] Though Truman was reportedly "shocked," he backed down right away.[57]

This case proved the value of an independent judiciary, especially considering that the first judge ever to review the matter (a Truman appointee) made the somewhat startling decision not to issue a restraining order. Apparently, his view of executive power under the Constitution was gravely different than that of the Supreme Court.

Both the North Carolina attachments dispute and Truman's attempted seizure of America's steel mills hinged on the interference of an executive (or monarch) in private commerce. In the earlier case, King George wanted to strip North Carolinians of their protections against being cheated out of money by debtors in England. Nearly two hundred years later, President Truman wanted to make himself the biggest steel baron in America to support a war he started without a declaration from Congress. Fortunately our independent judiciary was firmly established to prevent the abuse of power in the latter case. The colonists of early North Carolina would have been proud.

It was not a mere fluke of history that it was their property rights on which the North Carolinians chose to take such a forceful stand against the Crown. They were willing to engage in brinksmanship with a much more powerful force in order to make sure their courts enforced their property rights. Did they all read their Locke and understand their guaranteed rights to life, liberty, and property? Certainly not. But they understood their natural right to have their property respected, and they knew that if the rule of law were to be followed, their courts must uphold those property rights.

This same impulse has not diminished among American citizens today. When we seek to limit government's reach, we send a clear signal that whenever government strikes at a core value and threatens a key individual right, the people will respond. Even if government's encroachment seems mild at first, the people are right to push back. For the legislators of colonial North Carolina, the issue was not just the "Attachment Clause"—it was what it represented. It should have been easy to work out a fair fix for the law with the authorities in London. But what the royal government did was what governments unfortunately tend to do when they are challenged—they dug in. Whether or not the issue was truly critical, they sought to exercise their power because they *could*. Because the British Empire was a superpower.

They would learn, of course, that even a superpower is no match for ideas like rights and principles. And one of the most shocking demonstrations of the power of these ideas hit the British where it really hurt—their pocketbooks. The British fueled the expansion of their empire with taxation, with the successful colonies in North America a prime target for government shakedowns.

North Carolina was not the only place where colonists were at a tipping point over violations of their rights. Not long after their elected representatives took their stand in December 1773, another blow for political and economic freedom was struck by fellow colonists to the north.

CHAPTER FIVE

Tea Leaves in the Harbor

For imposing Taxes on us without our Consent . . .

BOSTON, MASSACHUSETTS
September 29, 1773

ANY INFORMED COLONIST WHO OPENED THE SEPTEMBER 29, 1773, edition of the *Massachusetts Gazette* would find a report that would make his blood boil. The paper carried the news that between three hundred and six hundred chests of tea were headed for Boston. This was no ordinary shipment, however. The paper also commented, "We are assured the above is a scheme of Lord North's," King George III's prime minister.[1]

A heavy tax on tea had been imposed on the colonies in His Majesty's name by the British Parliament—where the American colonists held no seats. The colonists maintained that this taxation without representation was a violation of their rights. The uproar spread through the major port cities. In Philadelphia, an anonymous writer using the pen name of Scaevola declared the approach of the tea "the most dangerous stroke, that has been ever meditated against the liberties of America." Scaevola castigated the officials of the East India Company in America directly: "You are marked out as political Bombardiers to demolish the fair structure of American liberty."[2]

As a result of this uproar, the Ports of Philadelphia and New York had already rejected shipments of British tea, leaving Boston as the only entry point for this cargo. But Boston was also proving inhospitable. "It is much to be wished," the *Massachusetts Gazette* urged Bostonians in September, "that the Americans will convince Lord North, that they are not ready to have the yoke of slavery rivetted about their necks, and send back the tea from whence it came."[3] When the tea shipments arrived, the Bostonians would be ready.

GRIFFIN'S WHARF, BOSTON, MASSACHUSETTS
December 16, 1773

The winter nights in Boston were usually cold but quiet, as citizens sought shelter indoors, kindling fires and huddling under quilts to stay warm.

On any other night, the last of the merchants from nearby Faneuil Hall would have already begun packing away their goods and returning home to their families. The children carousing in the streets would have been called home to dinner, as the New England darkness quickly engulfed the streets. Down at the harbor, the great wooden ships, waiting to sail for ports around the world, would have been rocking quietly in the harbor as gentle waves pushed them up and back against the docks.

Three of these vessels in particular were loaded with special cargo that would soon fill the shops of Boston and line the pockets of British merchants—fresh tea leaves from the British East India Company. On any other night, the *Dartmouth*, the *Beaver*, and the *Eleanor* would have sat peacefully, disturbed only by the occasional gust of wintry wind.

But this wasn't a typical winter night in Boston. The tea shipments, part of what the *Gazette* had called Lord North's "scheme," had arrived, and the town was preparing its response. The citizens had protested to British officials for weeks in an attempt to turn the merchant ships around and return them to London. But the bureaucracy—as is its nature—was at a standstill. Without the approval of the royal governor of the Massachusetts Bay Colony, the three ships could not leave the harbor until they were unloaded. To disobey the order would risk being fired upon by British troops. The deadline set by law for unloading the tea—December 17— was now approaching.[4]

On the sixteenth, more than a third of the city's residents— some five thousand people—gathered at the Old South Meeting House to call for their removal from the harbor. Despite the size of the meeting house, colonists were still overflowing into the street, trying to peer into the great hall.

After weeks of debate, the throngs had gathered to hear the answer from the final plea laid before the royal governor, Thomas Hutchinson. Francis Rotch, the owner of the *Dartmouth*, had gone before Hutchinson to request that the governor make an exception and allow the tea ships to leave the harbor without unloading.

Rotch walked silently through the door as a hush fell over the restless citizens. Now, at last, would come the conclusion to weeks of outcry and dissent. He stood at the front of the room. His face was visibly distraught; he too could not escape the feeling of uncertainty that pervaded the room. He announced that Governor Hutchinson had denied his request to exit the harbor and that he would be forced to unload the tea and pay the taxes by the next day. The room erupted into cries of shock and frustration.

The news provoked a group of patriotic citizens who called themselves the Sons of Liberty to make a final effort to stop the tea from being landed. According to some accounts, it was Samuel Adams himself who gave the word for the Sons of Liberty to begin their operation at Griffin's Wharf. After Rotch concluded his report, Adams rose up and shouted: "This meeting can do nothing more to save the country!" A nineteenth-century historian, George Bancroft, claims this was a covert order to the Sons of Liberty to exit the building and put their plan into action.

A group of men in costume—dressed as Native Americans— was set to board the three tea ships and destroy the cargo.[5] Samuel Adams and the other patriot leaders—well known to the British—could claim ignorance while their foot soldiers, upon getting the word from the Meeting House, donned their costumes and marched to the wharf. Between six and seven o'clock, the men boarded the *Dartmouth,* the *Beaver,* and the *Eleanor,* then took hold of the crates of British tea and began to throw them overboard. More than ninety thousand pounds of tea leaves seeped into the waters of Boston Harbor that night, as citizens cheered and British soldiers watched in horror. The next day, the *Boston Gazette* reported the protest with a sense of exuberance:

A number of brave & resolute men, determined to do all in their power to save their country from the ruin which their enemies had plotted, in less than four hours, emptied every chest of tea on board the three ships . . . amounting to 342 chests, into the sea . . . without the least damage done to the ships or any other property . . . the people are almost universally congratulating each other on this happy event.[6]

The Sons of Liberty risked their lives that night to stand against an overbearing King and Parliament. The amount of danger they faced was later made clear by Admiral Montague of the Royal Navy, who stated in his report: "I could easily have prevented the execution of this plan, but must have endangered the lives of many innocent people by firing upon the town."

This protest struck not only at an unjust tax but also at government intervention in the free market. The Townshend Acts of 1767 imposed a duty on imported tea and granted the East India Company a state-sponsored monopoly over the tea trade with America. The British Parliament, where the colonists were not represented, had effectively utilized taxes and duties to undersell and undermine the private enterprises of American colonists.[7]

This, however, was not the first time the British government decided to levy an unfair and unjust tax against the American colonists. This was part of a series of acts and decrees that had pushed the patriots to the brink of hostility, starting with the Stamp Act. With the passage of the Stamp Act in 1765, the colonists were forced to pay a tax on every sheet of paper printed in the colonies.

When prominent colonists like Patrick Henry decried the act as "Taxation without Representation," the author of the Stamp Act, Thomas Whately, argued that the colonists did not need to be directly represented in Great Britain to pay taxes. In the British Whig tradition, the right to vote was not connected to the ability of the King and Parliament to impose a tax.[8] Their claim was that the King and Parliament were the representatives of the entire empire, and they would do what was best for all citizens and colonists.

But the colonists had other ideas. Stephen Hopkins, elected governor of the Rhode Island colony and eventual signer of the Declaration of Independence, refuted British thinkers like Whately. In 1764, he published *The Rights of the Colonies Examined*, where he asserted that the colonists were subject only to the laws that they had consented to, therefore they could not be obligated "to part with their property."[9] Even further, he questioned the efficiency of taxation in the first place: "The parliament, it is confessed, have power to regulate the trade of the whole empire; and hath it not full power, by this means, to draw all the money and all the wealth of the colonies into the mother country?"[10] If the empire wanted to encourage prosperity for their subjects, he argued that taxation of the colonies was not the way to accomplish this goal—rather, greater trade should be encouraged to naturally grow the economies of both. Hopkins knew that this tyrannical taxation was not only morally wrong but also more economically destructive than a policy that could seek to promote more open trade between the colonies, Great Britain, and other nations.

This fight against rampant taxation carried on by Hopkins and others in the 1760s carried into the next decade, culminating on the night of the Boston Tea Party. The pamphlet elevated Stephen

Hopkins's ideas beyond Rhode Island, spreading them far and wide. One New York merchant remarked that *The Rights of the Colonies Examined* "meets the highest approbation, and even admiration, of the inhabitants of this city."[11] It was the ideals of freedom and opposition to taxation expressed by thinkers like Hopkins that gave birth the Sons of Liberty in 1765. Though the patriots eventually pushed Parliament to repeal the Stamp Act after one year, the Townshend Acts proved that King George III and his Parliament would not end their attempts to restrict trade and implement taxes over the colonists.

A new tax on tea in 1773 was seen by the patriots as an attempt to reinstitute the unsuccessful and illegitimate taxation policy created by British aristocrats, just as Whately sought to do with the Stamp Act. The polemicist Scaevola of Philadelphia—whose work was reprinted in the *Boston Gazette*—made the linkage clear: "The Stamp and Tea Laws were both designed to raise a revenue, and to establish parliamentary despotism, in America."[12]

By the time Bostonians met in the Old South Meeting House to protest the tea at Griffin's Wharf and the taxes that came with it, they were well aware that if they did not take a stand, the unfair policies would keep coming. As Scaevola pointed out: "If parliament can of right tax us 10 [pounds] for any purpose; they may of right tax us 10,000, and so on, without end." And this wasn't just about taxes: ". . . if we allow them a fair opportunity of pleading precedent by a successful execution of the tea act . . . we may bid adieu to all that is dear and valuable amongst men."[13]

As far back as 1764, colonial leaders like Stephen Hopkins understood that trade and economic growth were better routes to prosperity than taxation. His dissent upheld the idea not only that one must be properly represented to consent to a tax, but also that free trade was a pillar of liberty.

Similarly, the early American patriots understood that rampant taxation by the King and Parliament allowed the government in London to exploit their colonies. The economic situation in Great Britain was reeling after the large amount of debt incurred in connection with wars with France and other colonial powers. National debt in the mother country had soared to record levels.[14] The colonies, meanwhile, had an abundance of resources and land that could prove not only profitable, but potentially capable of bailing out the British Empire. To the American colonists, this relationship was obviously inequitable. The faraway government of King George III sought to use taxes on Americans to refill the coffers of the royal treasury. But this left the average colonist, who was still a British citizen, stuck with the burden of paying taxes imposed by lawmakers who were not accountable to him.

If thinkers like Hopkins recognized the threat of unjust taxation, it was leaders like Samuel Adams and the Sons of Liberty who recognized that the threat would always reemerge. Like the heads of a Hydra, when one is removed, two take its place. The Boston Tea Party was not an impromptu demonstration against the government, conducted out of blind public anger.[15] It was a methodical and planned act of civil disobedience, a last resort, a plan carried out because the Sons of Liberty foresaw the unwillingness of their rulers to give in to the demands of justice. Even if they managed to defeat this unjust act, they knew their war against tyranny would continue.

The Hydra of unjust taxation by a strong central government is alive today, and its heads are now innumerable. After the Revolution, Thomas Paine wrote in 1791's *Rights of Man*:

. . . we still find the greedy hand of government thrusting itself into every corner and crevice of industry. . . . Invention is continually exercised to furnish new pretences for revenue and taxation. It watches prosperity as its prey, and permits none to escape without a tribute.[16]

————

The stories of unjust tax hikes slapped on industrious people by a bloated central government echo into our own era. We may not be bailing out the government for a costly imperial war with France, but instead we are forced to cover the cost of wasteful programs and gradual expansion of the administrative state. A powerful government with the ability to tax naturally gravitates toward "prosperity as its prey." Congress and the executive branch have continually proved Thomas Paine correct.

From the later twentieth century until today, excessive taxes have been increasingly levied upon American families, all in the interest of lining the pockets of a debt-stricken federal government. For example, the Parent Tax Penalty forces parents to pay Social Security and Medicaid taxes on income, then pay to raise their children as citizens who also pay into entitlement programs. Taxes latch onto the economic engine of the family unit and cause a drag, forcing parents to essentially pay taxes twice for choosing to raise children.

But this is just one example of the countless ways that our overly complicated tax code has placed the burden of supporting a voracious central government onto the taxpayers of today. The federal tax code has grown *187 times longer* than it was in 1913. Today, we have more than seventy-four thousand pages of tax laws that demand the transfer of hard-earned money to the federal government.[17]

Perhaps the most concerning development in this realm is that both Congress and the presidency have been responsible for the expansion of taxes that encroach on our liberty. In the Declaration of Independence, Jefferson placed the blame for taxes on King George III. After all, it was King George who enabled these taxes to be imposed on the colonists. But the Parliament that drafted and passed these acts cannot escape blame. In Britain, the legislative body and the executive worked in tandem to enact and enforce policies like the Stamp Act.

The U.S. Constitution states in Article II, Section 1, Clause 1 that all bills that raise revenue for the federal government must originate in the House of Representatives. However, in the post–New Deal era, the executive branch has amassed enough power that it wields unilateral authority in many areas, including the power to impose tariffs! Our legislative branch is constitutionally supposed to hold the power of the purse and thereby keep taxation vested in the branch closest to the people—and the most *accountable* to the people. If citizens don't like the way their senator or representative is spending their money, they can vote them out of office in two or six years. No such accountability exists among unelected bureaucrats, of course. And the unchecked growth of the administrative state nestled within the executive branch, staffed by those unaccountable bureaucrats, has led to unfortunate fiscal consequences—from Franklin Roosevelt's welfare state expansion to the more recent tax increases under Obamacare.

When the Sons of Liberty marched to Griffin's Wharf, they were fighting against tyranny through taxation. With every new tax, we move away from that legacy. Rather than recommitting the mistakes of British tax master Thomas Whately, Washington, DC, needs to look to the words of men like Thomas Paine and Stephen Hopkins, who warned us to keep government out of our pockets.

By the same token, a free people have the right to conduct business however they see fit (subject, of course, to the rule of law). This is a key tenet of the economic freedom that the Boston Tea Party demonstration was meant to promote. And during the Revolution, the Founders made clear that their new nation would be a freely trading nation—a radical new step that amounted to a declaration of economic independence from Britain even before political independence was voted on. Unjust taxes like those on tea had many implications for overseas trade, and they roused many rebels across the colonies.

CHAPTER SIX
Trade Wars

For cutting off our Trade with all Parts of the
World . . .

CHARMING POLLY CHARGED TOWARD HER DESTINATION, A small but proud vessel, stout enough to handle the passage down the American Atlantic coast but fast enough to swiftly ply her trade among the many ports and inlets of the West Indies, where hopping from one island to another often meant anchoring under the flag of a different country—of Britain, the Netherlands, France, or Spain. The collection of islands from Cuba to Trinidad, slung in a loose line between the Spanish colonies in Florida and South America, were outposts of all the great powers of Europe. For an adventurer from the American colonies, there was hardly a more exciting place anywhere in the known world.

It was just such an adventurer who stood at the bow of the *Charming Polly*, his hand on the jib sheet—a line attached to the foremost sail—and his foot planted firmly at the base of the bowsprit, which sliced out into the clear blue sky ahead. Captain Thomas Truxtun, who had spent much of his life at sea since the age of twelve, was now, at the age of twenty, finally in command of his own ship. From his home port in New York City, he had already made two successful voyages to the Caribbean and back. But this third time would prove to be anything but charmed: Truxtun would end up a prisoner of His Majesty's Navy.

Captain Truxtun's first voyage to Jamaica had been a straightforward one. In the spring of 1775, according to historian Eugene Ferguson, trade between the American colonies and the West Indies was "exceptionally brisk."[1] The American merchants would sail down with "products of farm and of forest"—like meat, corn, flour, and rough timber—and return from the islands with rum, molasses, sugar, and more exotic woods like mahogany. Although some products had been voluntarily banned by the colonists themselves through Nonimportation Agreements—designed to keep money out of London merchants' pockets—seagoing tradesmen like Truxtun could still earn a solid living.[2]

While Truxtun was at sea on his first voyage, British Regulars clashed with Massachusetts militiamen at Lexington and Concord, and the dispute between Great Britain and her American colonies turned from a war of words into an armed conflict. Truxtun caught up with the news upon returning to New York in July 1775, and he immediately threw himself, his skills, and his ship into the service of the patriot cause. He set sail for Hispaniola, the large Caribbean island under French control in its west and

Spanish control in its east—colonies that would grow into the modern nations of Haiti and the Dominican Republic. At Hispaniola, Truxtun loaded up the *Charming Polly* with gunpowder—precious to the fledgling American military effort—and sailed for home.[3] He had officially become a rebel smuggler.

Those in command of the British ship now bearing down on him off St. Eustatius had no way of knowing that. They had no way of knowing, for instance, that this voyage saw him headed to the neutral Dutch island in search of more gunpowder, and guns too if he could find them.[4] He had not even reached the island to seek out this illicit cargo. As far as the British knew, he was a simple merchant from the colonies, minding his own business. They had no right to detain him, did they?

Technically, they did.

On December 22, 1775, Parliament had passed the American Prohibitory Act, the latest in a series of trade restrictions designed to use purse strings to strangle the rebelliousness out of the American colonies. Earlier that year, in March and April, Parliament had passed the Restraining Acts, which aimed to restrict the colonies to trade only with Great Britain and other British possessions. His Majesty's Government did not want meddlesome foreign powers like the French providing funds through trade, knowing that such funds might ultimately end up supporting the American rebels. Initially the Restraining Acts covered only the New England colonies, but a second incarnation was soon passed, extending the restrictions to cover most of the other colonies as well. After a few months, the Restraining Acts were superseded by the even more draconian Prohibitory Act.

"Be it therefore declared and enacted by the King's most excellent majesty," this new law announced, ". . . that all manner of trade is and shall be prohibited with the colonies . . . and that all ships and vessels of or belonging to the inhabitants of the said colonies, together with their cargoes . . . shall become forfeited to his Majesty, as if the same were the ships and effects of open enemies."[5] This law authorized the Royal Navy to seize American ships, and even capture any vessel coming into or out of an American port. All American seafarers were now "open enemies," including Thomas Truxtun.

Now on his third voyage to the West Indies, Truxtun was armed with a well-earned confidence that he could handle nearly anything the sea could throw at him. In many ways, his sailing career had begun like a great many sea stories, real and fictional. Born in the colony of New York, he lost his father at a young age and was sent to live with a family friend in the part of Long Island known as Jamaica (from a local Native American word meaning "beaver," having nothing to do with the Caribbean island).[6] But by his twelfth year, "the kindling spark of that spirit"—according to an early biography—"which has since shone so conspicuously in his character, led him to the sea."[7]

He spent a few years learning the ways of the mariner, sailing on merchant ships to Britain and back, until at the age of sixteen he found himself in a very different kind of service. It was the practice of the British Royal Navy in those days to "press"—forcibly compel into service—civilian sailors to fill berths on their warships. Truxtun was "pressed" and brought aboard the HMS *Prudent*, a ship of the line sporting sixty-four guns. The teenager's "intelligence and activity" were noticed by the British captain, who "endeavored to prevail on him to remain in the service," recognizing that he could have a brilliant career ahead of him as a naval officer.[8] But Truxtun was an entrepreneurial sort and had his eye on the greater fortunes to be made trading on the sea lanes. He took advantage of the earliest opportunity to leave the Royal Navy and return to merchant shipping. A few years later, he was master and part owner of the *Charming Polly*. And in April 1775, just six weeks after getting married, the young man from Jamaica, Long Island, had set sail on a voyage to Jamaica in the Caribbean—his first journey on his own ship.[9]

By January 1776 he had gained much experience from his first two voyages, knew the territory well. His ports of call were to be the British islands of Antigua and St. Christopher (commonly known as St. Kitts) and the nearby Dutch island of St. Eustatius. He knew the waters well, and his expert seamanship and capable command of his crew had made for a swift, uneventful voyage— just as Captain Truxtun liked it.

"A ship to larboard, sir!"

The cry from one of his crewmen snapped Truxtun to attention. He had been looking to starboard, to the right of the ship, and following the outstretched finger of the sailor who had run up to join him, turned his gaze to the left, or larboard. He had to squint and shield his eyes from the sun, but eventually he saw her— two masts at least, probably one of the larger Caribbean merchant vessels. Hardly a threat, except in the commercial sense. Still, it never hurt to be wary on the high seas.

"Keep an eye on her," Truxtun ordered his crewman. "Aye, sir," came the prompt reply, and Truxtun headed aft toward his cabin to fetch his spyglass. His well-traveled sea legs gave him no trouble walking across the deck, but as he sifted among his belongings looking for the spyglass, he heard a cry from another shipmate that made his stomach contract.

"She looks to be flying the red ensign, sir!"

Truxtun hurried back out onto the deck, steadied himself against the rail, and held the spyglass to his eye. The gentle rolling of the ship meant it would take him a few seconds to focus, but soon, there she was in the center of his field of view. She had not two masts but three, and gun ports all along her side—a warship, a frigate by the looks of her. As he shifted the spyglass to take in the whole view, he saw what he had been dreading. From her stern she flew a red flag with a Union Jack in the upper left corner: the battle flag of the Royal Navy.

Truxtun cursed himself silently for not spotting her sooner. Maybe she had been hiding in a bay, partially hidden by the hilly point of land at the northern tip of St. Eustatius. But what was a British warship doing lurking around Dutch territory? She was probably based in the British harbor at St. Kitts. Truxtun's mind was beginning to race into high gear, but with time-tested effort he calmed it down. He had nothing to fear. Not yet, anyway.

Aboard the *Charming Polly*, Truxtun had a decision to make. The British warship had clearly spotted him and was bearing down fast in his direction. The *Charming Polly* was smaller and lighter. As it was, Truxtun had the weather gauge—if he caught the wind just right, he might be able to outrun the heavier frigate. But there were still those guns . . . all the King's ship had to do was pull herself into cannon range and let off a broadside. One nine-pound ball of iron round shot in the right spot would send the *Charming*

Polly to the bottom of the Caribbean, likely with captain and crew along with it. Truxtun was, as the old sailors said, "caught between the devil and the deep blue sea."

The frigate was within hailing distance now, and one of her officers was shouting at the *Charming Polly* using a speaking trumpet. His words were carried by the wind in snatches at first, but soon they were close enough that his message came through clearly:

"This is His Majesty's ship *Argo*. In the name of King George, heave to at once!"

They were too close now. No time to run. Truxtun turned to his men. "Steady, lads," he said. If he projected calm to the crew, perhaps he'd start to feel that way himself. After all, he'd dealt with the Royal Navy before. "Let's heave to and see what they want." With a wry smile, he added, "Perhaps they'd just like to buy some tea!"

His men chuckled, but they understood what the command "heave to" meant and jumped into action. Some men eased the mainsail while others backed the jib to the windward side, and the helmsman steered the ship into the wind—all with the object of bringing the sloop almost to a complete stop. The *Argo* was nearly alongside them now. Truxton could see her officers in blue coats and cocked hats gathered on the quarterdeck, and redcoat Royal Marines armed with muskets lined up along her rail. The gun ports were open, too—twelve nine-pound cannons were pointed right at the *Charming Polly*.

Truxtun knew the routine. When he observed her sailors preparing to lower a boat into the water, he went into his cabin to get his ship's papers. By the time he came back on deck, the boat had rowed the short distance between the two vessels, and a British officer was calling for the captain to lower himself down. With a final wink at his crewmen, Thomas Truxtun, sheaf of papers tucked under his arm, climbed down the ladder and greeted the officer politely. A few short oar strokes later, he was roughly hoisted onto the deck of the *Argo* and presented to Captain William Garnier of His Majesty's Navy.

The *Argo* had first put to sea in 1759, and it was nearing the end of its service life. In less than a year, in fact, she would end up scrapped back in England. Named for the ship that carried Jason and his comrades in Greek mythology on their quest for the Golden Fleece, this *Argo* had indeed also chased riches—once helping to capture a Spanish galleon off the Philippines with a cargo worth some $1.5 million.[10] Now, in her twilight years, she was cruising the Caribbean on the hunt for smaller prey.

Her captain, William Garnier, was a veteran commander with plenty of Caribbean service under his belt. He was a consummate professional—just the sort of officer Truxton had served under during his brief Royal Navy tenure, and exactly the kind of man with whom he knew how to deal. Or so he thought.

He greeted Garnier respectfully as a fellow mariner and presented his papers, knowing them to be all in order—so he was shocked when the captain informed him that his ship would nonetheless be impounded in the naval dockyard at St. Kitts. Truxton protested, but Garnier was unmoved.[11]

"The Colony of New York is in rebellion, sir, and therefore this is a rebel ship," the British captain explained in calm, officious tones. "You have no choice but to proceed to St. Kitts under our escort." He paused, then added for emphasis: "Under our *guns*."

And so, Thomas Truxtun, on just his third voyage as a sea captain, was forced to sail the *Charming Polly* into St. Kitts harbor and surrender her to the British authorities. He was a victim of the King's trade restrictions on American colonists, "a commander with nothing to command," as a later biographer puts it.[12] The *Pennsylvania Gazette* of February 21, 1776, citing a January edition of a newspaper in Antigua, published a list of several ships seized by the Royal Navy over the previous few weeks and deposited in St. Kitts, including "Sloop Charming Polly, Thomas Truxton [*sic*] master, from New-York, brought in here by his Majesty's ship Argo, William Garnier, Esq; commander, the 2d January 1776."[13] Incidentally, the adjacent column carried an advertisement for "The New Edition of Common Sense" on sale from a Philadelphia printer. This was a pamphlet that was causing a great stir in the American colonies at the time, and of which we shall learn more later.

As luck would have it, it was to Philadelphia, rather than his home port of New York, that Thomas Truxtun would return after being stuck in the Caribbean for a few months following the loss of the *Charming Polly*. The war against the King was personal for him now, and he would go on to become one of the most distinguished officers in the early history of the United States Navy, eventually commanding the USS *Constellation*. But here our story must leave Captain Truxtun and look a few months backward toward the arguments that drove a trade debate in the body that was meeting at the time he made landfall in Philadelphia: the Continental Congress.

PHILADELPHIA

October 4, 1775

The crisp fall air brought a chill to Philadelphia and carried on it some of the withered leaves that had already left the trees. The occasional drafts that made their way into the meeting chamber at the State House, where the delegates of the Second Continental Congress had gathered, were especially welcome on this day—because the debate was getting heated.

"I should be for the resolutions about imports and exports standing till further order," announced Thomas Johnson of Maryland.

"The question," observed John Rutledge of South Carolina, "is whether we shall shut our ports entirely, or adhere to the Association. The resolutions we come to ought to be final." Another member objected that the North Carolina delegation was absent but expected shortly, so they had better hold off on a final vote.[14]

Sitting quietly at his desk, a pensive lawyer from Massachusetts, his brow furrowed in concentration, scribbled furiously with his pen. John Adams had a keen interest in trade policy, and—fortunately for history—was taking detailed notes on this debate.

The delegates were discussing how the united American colonies should conduct their trade with the rest of the world. Since 1774 they had been bound by the articles of the Continental Association, adopted by the First Continental Congress, which banned the purchase of goods from Great Britain. The Association had unified the various Nonimportation Agreements, which had sprung up in earlier years in different colonies, into a single cohesive policy. But in March 1775, Britain struck back with the Restraining Acts. The trade war between Britain and the American colonies was in full swing before the first shots of the Revolution rang out the following month.

On July 6, 1775, the Continental Congress issued their declaration on "the Causes and Necessity of their taking up Arms," authored primarily by Thomas Jefferson with the assistance of John Dickinson of Pennsylvania. Jefferson mentioned the boycott of British goods, stating, "We have even proceeded to break off our commercial Intercourse with our Fellow Subjects," calling this "the last peaceable Admonition, that our Attachment to no Nation upon Earth should supplant our Attachment to Liberty." Jefferson and Dickinson also attacked the trade restrictions imposed by the Restraining Acts, noting that "the commercial Intercourse of whole Colonies, with foreign Countries, and with each other, was cut off by an Act of Parliament" and that "several of them [the New England colonies] were entirely prohibited from the Fisheries in the Seas near their Coasts, on which they always depended for their Sustenance."[15]

Now, with the summer turned into fall, the delegates were trying to decide whether their trade should be expanded or contracted, as the conflict with Britain showed no signs of abating.

Silas Deane of Connecticut raised an important point: the necessity of bringing in ammunition through trade. "Whether we are to trade with all nations except Britain, Ireland and the West Indies, or with one or two particular nations," Deane observed, "we cannot get ammunition without allowing some exports." He further explained that trading physical commodities was the colonies' only option, as the colonial money they printed for themselves would not be accepted elsewhere.[16]

Robert Livingston of New York, whose very prominent family had been granted an estate known as Livingston Manor by the first King George, rose to hold forth after Deane. "We should go into a full discussion of the subject," he implored his colleagues. "Every gentleman ought to express his sentiments." He then proceeded to express his own view that an expansion of trade would be in everyone's best interest. "We have nothing to fear but disunion among ourselves," he observed. "What will disunite us, more than the decay of all business? The people will feel, and will say that Congress tax them and oppress them worse than Parliament." He then moved on to military concerns—"ammunition cannot be had unless we open our ports"—before reaching his conclusion: "I am for doing away our non-exportation agreement entirely. I see many advantages in leaving open the ports, none in shutting them up. I should think the best way would be to open all our ports."[17]

After Livingston's extended oration, Adams recorded that the debate continued mostly between Johnson, Rutledge, and Lee of Virginia. John Joachim Zubly, a minister representing Georgia, who had been born in Switzerland, tried to keep everyone on task by reminding the delegates: "The question should be whether the export should be kept or not." Unfortunately, he was met with a "rambling speech" by Samuel Chase of Maryland which, as later historians point out, "appear[ed] to argue on both sides of more than one of the questions at issue."[18]

The debate ended without a satisfactory conclusion as Edward Rutledge, John's brother, announced that he disagreed "with all who think the non exportation should be broke, or that any trade at all should be carried on," and Livingston declared that he was "not convinced by any argument."

The debate resumed the following day, October 5, and once again John Adams made notes of the proceedings. Christopher Gadsden took up the cause of his fellow South Carolina delegates, the Rutledge brothers, and sought to focus the question once again: "I wish we may confine ourselves to one point . . . whether we shall shut up all our ports, and be all on a footing."

Zubly, who had gathered his thoughts from listening to the previous day's debate, came out strongly against opening American ports, partly out of fear of Britain's renowned Royal Navy. "The Navy can stop our harbors and distress our trade," he cautioned, "therefore it is impracticable, to open our ports." He concluded his remarks by sounding a hopeful note of reconciliation with England: "I am clearly against any proposition to open our ports to all the world; it is not prudent to threaten; the People of England will take it we design to break off, to separate."[19] His caution about offending the mother country was consistent with his general opposition to independence. A few weeks after this debate, Zubly quit the Continental Congress and joined the loyalist cause.[20]

A few days later, in his lodgings, John Adams sat before his desk and poured out his thoughts on the trade issue in a letter to his friend James Warren, husband of the famous patriot writer Mercy Otis Warren. "A more intricate and complicated subject never came into any man's thoughts than the trade of America," Adams vented. "The questions that arise, when one thinks of it, are very numerous." But for Adams, they boiled down to one: "If we must have trade, how shall we obtain it?" He outlined a plan to bring more foreign merchants to America by advertisements and word of mouth, but he admitted that this depended on keeping American harbors safe for trade—"To talk of coping suddenly with [Great Britain] at sea would be Quixotic indeed."

A few months later, Thomas Truxtun would find out just how true that was.

PHILADELPHIA
April 1776

Much had changed since the contentious debates over trade in the fall of 1775. In late November of that year, Benjamin Franklin received intelligence from David Hartley, a Member of Parliament friendly to the American cause, that the prime minister, Lord North, was preparing to repeal the Restraining Acts passed some months before—not to loosen the British grip on American commerce but rather "to make way for a general bill including all America, and as I hear to make prizes of all American vessels that can be catched."[21] That rumor was proved true when the Prohibitory Act was passed, on December 22, 1775, and on January 2, 1776, Thomas Truxtun's *Charming Polly* was one of those American vessels unlucky enough to be "catched" by the Royal Navy.

In February, the Continental Congress found themselves once again debating whether or not to open American ports to foreign commerce. Some delegates still urged caution. James Wilson of Pennsylvania was not among them. Wilson was a Scotsman who had studied Adam Smith and other Scottish Enlightenment thinkers at the University of St Andrews.[22] Perhaps remembering Smith, he argued that merchants should be free to take risks in trading wherever they wanted. "I think the Merchants ought to judge for themselves of the danger and risk," he said. "Trade ought in war to be carried on with greater vigor."

Not everyone agreed. Roger Sherman of Connecticut argued that the risks were still too great: "We can't carry on a beneficial trade, as our enemies will take our ships. A treaty with a foreign power is necessary, before we open our trade, to protect it."

Meanwhile, Benjamin Harrison of Virginia fumed: "We have hobbled on under a fatal attachment to [Great Britain]. I felt it as much as any man but I feel a stronger to my country."[23] Harrison clearly thought of his "country" as something already separate and distinct from Britain.

His fellow Virginia delegate, George Wythe, evidently felt the same way. He rose next and made a stirring argument connecting the Americans' economic independence to their political independence. "Americans will hardly live without trade," he observed. He admitted there were obstacles to attracting foreign trade, but that the colonies themselves should be able to influence their own destiny. "Why," Wythe asked the chamber, "should we be so fond of calling ourselves dutiful subjects" of Great Britain? "If we should offer our trade to the Court of France, would they take notice of it, any more than if Bristol or Liverpool should offer theirs, while we profess to be subjects? No. We must declare ourselves a free people."[24]

Among colonial leaders, there was a growing sense that the

total economic separation from Great Britain brought about by the Prohibitory Act was driving the colonies' political separation as well. On March 23, 1776, John Adams put pen to paper to write to General Horatio Gates, and shared these observations:

> I know not whether you have seen the Act of Parliament called the restraining Act, or prohibitory Act, or piratical Act, or plundering Act, or Act of Independency, for by all these Titles is it called. I think the most [appropriate] is the Act of Independency, for King Lords and Commons have united in Sundering this Country and that I think forever. It is a complete Dismemberment of the British Empire. It throws thirteen Colonies out of the Royal Protection, levels all Distinctions and makes us independent in Spite of all our supplications and Entreaties.[25]

"It may be fortunate," Adams added, "that the Act of Independency should come from the British Parliament, rather than the American Congress," although he found it "very odd that Americans should hesitate at accepting Such a Gift from them."[26]

Richard Henry Lee similarly wrote in a letter back to Virginia that he found it "curious to observe that whilst people here are disputing and hesitating about independancy, the Court by one bold Act of Parliament, and by a conduct the most extensively hostile, have already put the two Countries asunder."[27]

Lee sent his letter on April 1, 1776, and just a few days later he and his fellow delegates gathered at the Pennsylvania State House to settle the trade issue for good. On April 3, it was ordered that the Congress devote special time as a "committee of the whole to take into consideration the trade of the United Colonies." That discussion was indeed held on the fourth, and Benjamin Harrison reported its results, but they were tabled until the next session. Because April 5 was Good Friday and Congress did not meet, with many members repairing to Philadelphia's various houses of worship, they next convened at ten on the morning of Saturday the sixth.

That morning, the Congress took a historic step toward America's economic—and eventually political—independence. They passed a resolution declaring that "any goods, wares, and merchandise" could be imported *and* exported "from the thirteen United Colonies, by the inhabitants thereof, and by the people of all such countries as are not subject to the King of Great Britain, to any parts of the world which are not under the dominion of the said King."[28] America's ports were officially open for business—to all nations except Great Britain.

Later that day, no doubt exhausted, John Adams stopped to record his own mixed opinions in his diary. "These Resolutions are on the Journal, and amount to something," he admitted. "They opened the Ports and set our Commerce at Liberty: But they were far short of what had been moved by Members from Massachusetts, Maryland and Virginia." He made sure to make special note of one of the resolutions passed: "Resolved that no Slaves be imported into any of the thirteen Colonies." Because the slave trade was mainly a British-run enterprise, the American colonies avoided it—at least temporarily—during the Revolution.[29]

Other delegates hurried to spread the word to their home

states and beyond. Elbridge Gerry of Massachusetts quickly dashed off a note to the president of his colony's Provincial Congress:

> Dear Sir,
>
> I have just time to send you by the post a newspaper, in which is inserted the resolves of Congress for opening of American Ports to all nations except such as are subject to the King of Great Britain. It is a matter of importance that these resolves should be published in all the papers, and sent to every part of Europe and the West-Indies not inimical to the colonies.[30]

A letter from Joseph Hewes of North Carolina showed how close to home this issue came. "A 44 gun ship lies in the bay [near] the Capes and has taken several vessels," he reported, before noting that "Congress has agreed to open the Trade."[31]

————

The firsthand experience of Captain Truxtun and the debates of the Continental Congress show how critical trade was to the eventual independence of the American colonies. When the colonies banded together to limit their trade with Britain, and later to revamp their trade policy in the face of aggression from London, they demonstrated the power of international trade to drive policy in other areas. They were fed up with the Crown intruding on their affairs, whether by interfering with their laws, their courts, or their trade.

Of course, it isn't only goods that move back and forth along trade routes. The American colonies were constantly importing new ideas as well, which came along with the new settlers who brought their skills and talents from the old world to the new. One such individual was Thomas Paine, a classic example of an intellect that could not be bound by the rigid social structures of England but who seemed tailor-made for revolutionary America. Indeed, Paine helped give revolutionary America its voice.

CHAPTER SEVEN
A Revolution in the Minds of the People

Nothing can settle our affairs so expeditiously as an open and determined declaration for independence.

—THOMAS PAINE, *COMMON SENSE*

SOMEWHERE IN THE NORTH ATLANTIC
November 1774

THE SHIP CAREENED THROUGH THE ICY TWENTY-FOOT WAVES, tossing about barrels, pots, and people. Doing everything he could to keep the fever mixed with seasickness at bay, the weary passenger put his head back on the pillow on his bunk. He shivered and pulled the blanket as tightly as he could. His mind drifted. He thought back to his childhood—an idyllic one, really. The memories of the thatched cottage of his parents. The cows grazing in the rolling pastures that surrounded his village of Thetford, northeast of London. His father was a modest Quaker artisan who made ropes and ladies' corsets out of whale bones.[1] His mother was a gentle Anglican homemaker. Thoughts of their smiling faces were comforting inside the dank, dark hull of a rocking vessel that might turn out to be a death trap.

But as much as he tried to keep his thoughts focused on cheerful reminiscences, Thomas Paine couldn't shake the hatred of his youth. It was a rage that filled him every time he thought back to his early years. The memory that stung most involved the hill that overlooked his family cottage. Known as "The Wilderness," it was where peasants were hanged regularly. They included family friends, and a young boy who had merely stolen a penknife. Women were regularly stoned to death.[2] And each spring, a new round of peasants would be executed there, almost as a kind of sport for the local officials. The aristocrats would gather, wagering on how long it would take those hanging by a noose to finally succumb. Those memories had stuck with Paine, as had the rage against the injustice they engendered.

The nausea was coming back. Paine gripped the side of his bunk. With all the strength he could muster, he pulled his torso up so that he could vomit somewhere other than in his own bunk. As much as his fellow passengers didn't appreciate it, the floorboards were already soaked with all manner of fluids purged from bodies wracked by typhoid. A few already lay dead in their bunks.

In the throes of a blistering fever, Paine wasn't sure what had brought him to this frozen hell reeking of death in the middle of the North Atlantic. The stench of vomit and death permeated his nostrils and every part of his being. Some of his shipmates had long since expired, their corpses pitched overboard and consigned forever to a watery grave. At least they were out of their misery, Paine thought to himself.

As his fever broke, he then remembered who was responsible for his damnable predicament. Franklin. Benjamin Franklin. That rogue—a charismatic and lovable one though he was—had convinced him to abandon England, with its injustice and aristocracy, for the colonies. Though Paine hadn't been successful at keeping a job (father's apprentice, privateer, tax collector, teacher), or his wives for that matter (losing his first to childbirth, his second to divorce), Franklin saw in the penniless man an undeniable intellect and fiery rhetorician with a passion for justice and equality, all traits that could serve him well in a place like America.

Franklin directed Paine to his own hometown of Philadelphia. And so Paine sold everything he owned at auction to pay off his debts and hitch a ride aboard a ship headed west. With the might of his pen and a fresh start, Franklin had no doubt that the thirty-seven-year-old man could change his ill fortune. Maybe he could even change the world. But first, he would need to survive the rest of the journey.

Paine's mind drifted off again, this time into a long, deep sleep.

PHILADELPHIA
January 24, 1775

Paine held in his hands the fruits of his labor in the faint glow of a candle. The night was inky black, the windows shut tight against the driving snow. With the pride of a new father, he stroked the handsome blue cover and leafed through the pages with his ink-stained hands. "A magazine," he would say, "is the nursery of genius."

The debut issue of *Pennsylvania Magazine* had been his responsibility as the new publication's executive editor. Its motto, *Fuval in sylvis habilare* ("Happy it is to live in the woods"), was emblazoned on the cover. The words matched how the broke Quaker felt about his adopted home, whose name translated to "Penn's Woods." To Paine, even bustling Philadelphia felt like a sprawling wilderness compared with the people-choked streets of London.

It had taken a full six weeks in Pennsylvania for Paine to feel well enough to begin work after his wretched voyage. He had disembarked from the vessel barely able to walk. But as soon as he staggered off the dock and his feet touched the cobblestones of Philadelphia's streets, his recovery—and his love affair with America—began.

Paine's hatred for monarchy burned even more fiercely in his new home than it had back in England. He had settled in Philadelphia at his friend Benjamin Franklin's urging. As he sought out work—he intended to become a teacher or private tutor—he carried with him a letter of recommendation from Franklin. Though he was still living in London on a diplomatic mission from the colonies, Franklin was easily the city's most recognized citizen. His inventions and brilliant writings made him world famous. His dabbling in radical politics in London's elite clubs had brought him into contact with Paine. "The bearer Mr. Thomas Paine is very well recommended to me as an ingenious worthy young man," Franklin's letter read.

Philadelphia was the largest, wealthiest city in America. Like the nation that surrounded it, Philadelphians brimmed with hope and boundless ambition. Its grid of modern streets lent a sense of civility to an otherwise-bustling port city (one that was a hundred miles from the ocean but nonetheless the biggest in the world, after London and Liverpool).[3] The grid of streets, lit by whale-oil lamps, along with a library, hospital, and firehouse, was a bastion of civilization in the wilds. Like a reminder that man had not yet entirely conquered Mother Nature, pigs roamed the garbage-strewn streets. Mosquitoes congregated over pools of sewage.

All of this lent to the city a veneer of charm and a feeling of adventure for an expatriate British writer discovering his new home. Armed with a letter of recommendation from the city's most famous resident, Paine searched for work. He soon landed a job as the executive editor of the brand-new *Pennsylvania Magazine*.

PHILADELPHIA
April 23, 1775

News had just reached Philadelphia that British troops and colonial militias had exchanged fire at Lexington and Concord, a several days' ride away. The skirmish left men on both sides dead. Paine was outraged. There was no doubt about his loyalties. "When the country, into which I had just set my foot, was set on fire about my ears, it was time to stir. It was time for every man to stir," he wrote.[4] "Those who had been long settled had something to defend; those who had just come had something to pursue; and the call and the concern was equal and universal," he added.[5] Paine felt as one with his fellow Americans pushing for open rebellion.

Even with blood now shed, the idea of independence was still a taboo. If there was going to be a movement for independence or a war, it was more likely that it would be *between* the colonies than on behalf of all of them. The colonies had very little in common and represented a patchwork of classes, cultures, faiths, and traditions. They squabbled constantly. That the thirteen colonial governments could somehow put aside their differences and organize an independence movement when they hadn't ever done so was unlikely at best.

Still, a few brave voices pushed the boundaries of what was deemed acceptable political speech. John Adams, a representative of the Massachusetts militiamen killed at Lexington and Concord, moved to have every colony create its own local government and pushed for independence at the newly created Second Continental Congress. It was a radical position, one that made him "an object of nearly universal scorn and detestation," his friend and fellow representative Benjamin Rush recalled.[6] The Massachusetts governor was offering bounties of five hundred pounds (well over one hundred thousand dollars today) for the heads of rebels John Hancock and Samuel Adams.

Paine had better things to do than become an enemy of the Crown. After all, he had a fledgling magazine to tend. In the three months since its launch, the magazine had thrived. Eschewing controversial essays on politics and religion, *Pennsylvania Magazine* kept things light and optimistic. With new-invention announcements, mathematical puzzles, and images of maidens and flowers, the magazine was quintessentially American in its quirkiness, diversity, and idealism.

But beneath the sunny facade, Paine's magazine and adopted city kept a lid on a simmering rage. A pacifist Quaker though he was, Paine was breathing in the combustible air around him. British rule was becoming ever more insufferable. Throughout the 1760s, the Crown had increased its punitive taxes and duties with legislation such as the Stamp Act, the Sugar Act, and the taxes on tea. The King was sanctioning increasingly indefensible actions by British troops stationed in the colonies.

Worse still, and especially grating for Paine, was the undeniable attitude of superiority that British officials in the colonies took toward their citizens. They talked and walked among them as if they were "betters" over a crude mob of brutish American ruffians. There was nothing Paine loathed more than the remnants of the feudal system he had seen up close as a child in the British countryside. Now the British were trying to impose their rigid class system (which in many ways still exists today) on a land forged by the most unassuming and democratic of peoples, where a more egalitarian society might have a chance to flourish. Paine knew what it would mean if the aristocrats had their way in sullying America. He didn't want to see land, money, and power pass only from father to son, as he'd seen in his homeland. He thought back to the limp bodies swinging gently in the wind atop the hill behind his house.

The time for ignoring the increasingly volatile political situation was over—at least in Paine's mind. Over the objections of his employer, Thomas Aitken, Paine included increasingly incendiary essays in the magazine. Paine attacked the British and slaveholders in the South with increasing alacrity. He received hate mail in return. Paine wrote that the Americans' "attachment to Britain was obstinate, and it was at the time a kind of treason to speak against it. They disliked the ministry, but they esteemed the nation. Their idea of grievance operated without resentment, and their single object was reconciliation."[7]

Independence was still unthinkable. King George had declared the colonies to be in rebellion, but the Pennsylvania and New

Jersey Assemblies instructed their representatives at the Continental Congress to do nothing that would push them further away from the Crown. Even Paine's longtime friend Ben Franklin assured William Pitt back in London that no one "drunk or sober" across the Atlantic would dare favor breaking away.[8] Franklin overstated things to be sure, but even in 1775, there was no organized movement afoot toward independence.

Paine resolved to do something about it. So he set about writing.

PHILADELPHIA
January 10, 1776

Paine was quietly at work in his office, pen in hand. On his desk were Thomas Hobbes's *Leviathan* and an answer to it, John Locke's *An Essay Concerning Human Understanding*—both of which had shaped his views on the role of just government and its relationship with the people it governed. Locke's words had haunted Paine for years: "When a ruler stops maintaining the welfare of his subjects, when he wields the power of the government against the people, when he allows Parliament and his ministry to become corrupt and a foe of human liberty, he is nothing but a tyrant, and it is the people's right to remove him."[9] Was not King George the very sort of tyrant whom Locke portrayed? And if so, didn't the American people have a right to look for an alternative form of government?

Paine had a knack for blocking from his mind the steady din of morning foot traffic and drum of carriage wheels and horseshoes on cobblestones when he worked, but a loud rap at the door broke his concentration. It was Dr. Benjamin Rush—physician, writer, politician, man of letters, and one of Paine's closest associates this side of London. Rush had been urging Paine on his latest writing endeavor, and this time he came bearing the final fruits.

There in his outstretched hand were seventy-seven loosely bound pages. Rush had for months encouraged Paine to finally write a magnum opus—to channel the rage he felt after Lexington and Concord into a political treatise. Rush had become a de facto literary agent. When the manifesto was done, Rush had approached Philadelphia's top publishers, one by one, imploring them to make the words public.

None had the temerity to publish something so radical. After all, the pamphlet's author wasn't willing to affix his name to it; why should they? Publishing such an inflammatory tract could be construed as treason. They all passed. A Scottish printer on Third Street felt different. For taking such a risk, Robert Bell demanded half the profits and that Paine reimburse him if the pamphlet incurred any loss or legal liability. Paine could maintain his anonymity. The first edition, which Paine saw for the first time in Rush's hands, merely said "written by an Englishman."

This was not just another short magazine essay but rather a stand-alone work to be circulated on its own. Aside from newspapers and magazines, pamphlets had become the most popular form of publishing by the mid-eighteenth century, far cheaper and more accessible than books. At twenty-one thousand words, it had taken many weeks to write—weeks of agonizing late nights toiling away after finishing his full-time job at the magazine. Paine had included excerpts from his columns, but most of it was new and wholly original material. Like most everything he penned, Paine wrote it out by hand and then handed the scrawl to an assistant to typeset.

In the manner of lawyers and philosophers, these essays were typically carefully written and meticulously argued, drawing on obscure references to Tacitus and Montesquieu.[10] With this essay, there would be no mincing of words or the scholarship of Roman philosophers. This would be an impassioned barrage of words designed to stir hearts as much as minds. This was the language of the common people. It contained none of the lofty rhetoric taught in Latin classes at Harvard. There was no cover or binding, just pages sewn together, all for the price of a shilling.

For months, Paine's work had borne the working title *Plain Truth*. But now, in time for publication, he had settled on a name for his first pamphlet: *Common Sense*. Addressed directly to "the inhabitants of America," *Common Sense* was a plea for independence. "The cause of America is, in a great measure, the cause of all mankind," the essay began. The sentence was shocking in its grandiosity. Thirteen infant colonies would somehow determine the fate of all mankind?[11]

The words were ludicrous. But also prophetic.

MONTICELLO, ALBEMARLE COUNTY, VIRGINIA
February 1776

The office may have been lacking in physical size, but this was made up for by the ambition of its occupant. Indeed, the office was a testament to his vast and curious mind. A contraption that copied a handwritten note onto a separate paper—a primitive Xerox machine of sorts—sat on his desk. Strewn about were unanswered letters, books stacked high in at least five different languages, and maps depicting parts unknown. Outside the windows, the frost-bitten orchards of Monticello stretched to the foothills of the Shenandoah and on to the tidewaters of Virginia.

Hunched over his desk, Thomas Jefferson was working feverishly to attack the pile of work. His travels had taken him to Philadelphia through Christmas, and the 250-mile journey had been especially grueling in the January winter. As much as duty called, he was glad to be back at his home, among his books and gardens.

Work and correspondence from friends and fellow patriots had piled up in his absence. It had taken him longer than usual to get through his work. He had endured weeks of mind-bending migraines, which had been made worse by all of the travel. But he had been attending to important business. In Philadelphia there stirred talk of war—and even of independence.

As he sifted and sorted slowly through the letters, humming and singing as he always did when he read, he came across something new—a parcel from Thomas Nelson, a fellow Virginia delegate to the Continental Congress. "I send you," Nelson's letter said, "a present of 2/ worth of Common Sense."[12] Indeed, that was the pamphlet's title: *Common Sense.* Jefferson leaned back in his desk chair and began to read.

The plainspoken, egalitarian Englishman who barely survived his voyage to the New World had finally given voice to sentiments felt by hundreds of thousands in his adopted homeland. Almost overnight, it gave colonists the courage to voice opinions they hadn't dared to share in public. And its ideas had reached the very top of colonial society.

Common Sense was shared and reprinted faster than any publication in the history of the world. In proportion to America's population at the time (2.5 million), it remains our country's best-selling work. Within three months, one hundred thousand copies had been sold. After a year, sales were up to half a million. A comparably performing book in present-day America would be one that sold a staggering *12 million* copies in three months.[13] It was read repeatedly in churches and public meeting places, expanding its audience at least tenfold. The essay was eventually published in German, French, Polish, Dutch, and Russian, though most of the European editions carefully omitted any of Paine's denunciations of hereditary rule.

Paine's words had leaped off the page and into the national conversation. Though his name was left off at first (he allowed it to be attached to later editions and proudly claimed authorship after independence), his ideas were a topic of discussion in just about every tavern, church, and public square throughout the colonies. His pamphlet inspired hundreds like it, some arguing vociferously against it, others in support—and many thousands of responses in the pages of local newspapers. Everyone had an opinion. Soon too would a generation of Founding Fathers, who would have the courage to translate Paine's polemical work into a political document that would shake the world.

Common Sense was a forceful rejection of the hereditary rights that marked England's monarchy and aristocracy. Drawing on the examples of ancient Greece and Rome, Paine provided a new rationale for transmitting wealth and political power—a rationale based no longer on who your father was but instead on how hard you worked and how successful you were in persuading others to support you. It gave the language of republican democracy to colonists who read and shared the pamphlet with reckless abandon.

The essay convinced Americans that there could be life without a monarch. ("The king is not to be trusted without being looked after, or in other words, that a thirst for absolute power is the natural disease of a monarchy.") There was no such thing as the divine right of kings, Paine argued. ("One of the strongest natural proofs of the folly of the hereditary right in kings, is that nature disapproves it, otherwise she would not so frequently turn it into ridicule by giving mankind an ass for a lion.") The laws of nature and the Bible itself proved so. Only children needed governing by someone else; adults could rule themselves if they created laws that a government enforced. ("That so far as we approve of monarchy, that in America THE LAW IS KING.")

Paine was effectively offering a self-help guide for citizens. The residents of the colonies could wean themselves from the Crown if they so chose. The result wouldn't be anarchy but rather a government that reflected the American people's noblest ambitions. Kings had no special divine permission to rule over anyone else. Adults didn't need a fatherly monarch blessing their every move. They simply needed rule of law. They needed the ability to vote for their own leaders. Even the English system, which had some democratic protections for commoners, kept real power in the hands of the elites by virtue of a hereditary king and the nobility in the House of Lords. "For all men being originally equals," as Paine wrote in *Common Sense*, "no one by birth could have a right to set up his own family in perpetual preference to all others for ever."

More than that, Thomas Paine convinced Americans that theirs was not a traitorous cause but something much nobler. Their fight was nothing less than the struggle for English constitutional government dating back to the Magna Carta. They sought to reclaim the natural rights that God had bestowed on them and which King George had usurped. The basic liberty that let them engage in peaceful economic pursuits was hampered by excessive taxation. Furthermore, by subjecting the colonists to taxes approved by a Parliament in which they had no representation, the King was not deriving just powers from the consent of the people—he was acting unjustly.

He pointed out the paradox of the colonies' situation, which Americans had simply grown accustomed to. "There is something very absurd in supposing a continent to be perpetually governed by an island," he wrote. The status quo was unsustainable, and surely if America only took hold of its destiny from its imperial overlords, it could not only survive but thrive on its own.

The only solution, Paine maintained, was independence. "We have every opportunity and every encourage[ment] before us, to form the noblest, purest constitution on the face of the earth. We have it in our power to begin the world over again."

His words crystallized the thoughts of more and more Americans who no longer wanted a negotiated reconciliation with Britain but a divorce altogether. Within weeks of its publication, no fewer than ninety separate declarations of independence were made by localities up and down the Eastern Seaboard. What remained was whether the leaders of the Continental Congress would make a declaration of their own on behalf of all the colonies—a declaration of a new nation.

The book also found an audience with the delegates to the Second Continental Congress, on whom the burdens of separation from or reconciliation with the British Empire were especially heavy. Indeed, because the first edition was published anonymously, guessing the pamphlet's authorship soon became a parlor game among those who gathered at Philadelphia to debate the political future. "People Speak of it in rapturous praise," one of John Adams's friends wrote to him. Another speculated to him that Ben Franklin was the author. "I think I see strong marks of your pen in it," suggested a third. But Adams confided to his wife, "I could not have written any Thing in so manly and striking a style."[14]

"Have you seen the pamphlet *Common Sense*?" General Charles Lee wrote George Washington to ask. "I never saw such a masterly irresistible performance. . . . I own myself convinced, by the arguments, of the necessity of separation." Washington was impressed, enough so that for the first time he endorsed the idea of independence. The pamphlet, he readily admitted, was "sound doctrine and unanswerable reasoning [that] will not leave members [of Congress] at a loss to decide upon the propriety of separation. . . . [It is] a wonderful change in the minds of many men."[15] Even in his old age, Thomas Jefferson held the opinion that "no writer has exceeded Paine in ease and familiarity of style, in perspicuity of expression, happiness of elucidation, and in simple and unassuming language."[16]

Paine was different from almost all the Founding Fathers, who almost to a person were wealthy landowners: distinguished lawyers, traders, farmers, or plantation owners. Like his prose, most of Paine's political philosophy was raw, unsettling, and radical in its populism. His vision of democracy had no need for checks and balances; just the voice of the people.

Paine's radicalism was one reason why John Adams would

turn against him in later years. Indeed, he spoke for many of his colleagues when he later assessed that *Common Sense* was "so democratical, without any restraint or even an attempt at any equilibrium or counter poise, that it must produce confusion and every evil work." Adams had been the first and most outspoken of the Founders in favor of independence, but he would downplay Paine's role in making the idea broadly acceptable. "He is a keen Writer," Adams conceded, but *Common Sense* was nothing more than "a tolerable Summary of the Arguments which I had been repeating again and again in Congress for nine months."[17] Nearer to his death, Adams was less generous. The pamphlet was "a poor, ignorant, Malicious, short-sighted, Crapulous Mass." The second president maintained something of an unhealthy obsession with the man and his work. He would gripe to Jefferson, "History is to ascribe the American Revolution to Thomas Paine."[18]

In fact, early American history did not in fact ascribe much, if anything, to Thomas Paine. And that is a shame, because without him, independence would have come later, or perhaps not at all. Paine's role would be overshadowed by a generation that would include signers of the founding documents, presidents, vice presidents, chief justices, and the first elected representatives of an independent nation. Paine himself never sought, let alone attained, such positions.

Still, his importance cannot be understated, nor can the virtue of his example. Though he was among the poorest of the founding generation, he gave all the money—what would be equivalent to millions of dollars today—that he earned from the blockbuster sales of *Common Sense* to support George Washington's Continental Army. "As my wish was to serve an oppressed people, and assist in a just and good cause, I conceived that the honor of it would be promoted by my declining to make even the usual profits of an author," Paine later said.

He put his resources and even his life on the line to fight for the ideals he described in his writings. Many may have thought Paine a radical, but in reality there was nothing radical about the notion that every individual human soul yearns for freedom. Paine, who had witnessed firsthand the shackled stratification of a society where one's social position could determine the course of one's entire life, tapped into that yearning and gave voice to it in eloquent terms that have echoed all the way to the present day. He understood that the very basic principle of individual liberty was simple, powerful, and true enough that it could form the basis for a new nation. At a time when founding a country on an ideal was barely thinkable, Paine made it seem possible in clear, pointed prose. In doing so, he helped bring that idea from seeming to being and changed the course of history.

Thomas Paine may have kindled inspiration for the idea of independence, but the actual implementation of that idea would fall to others. Paine could give voice to the desires of many of Britain's North American colonists, but it was up to those colonists' elected representatives in the Continental Congress to handle the mechanics of that momentous change. And this was done through the distinctly *un*radical means of proper parliamentary procedure. Still, Paine's inspiration was clear; the politicians simply launched from the platform built by the polemicist.

On June 7, 1776, the Continental Congress took up *Common*

Sense as an official order of business. Richard Henry Lee of Virginia moved that Congress take up the pamphlet's recommendations to draft a new constitution, and of most significance, to draft what Paine called "a manifesto to be published"—one that would announce that "these United Colonies are, and of right ought to be, free and independent states, that they are absolved from all allegiance to the British Crown, and that all political connection between them and the state of Great Britain is, and ought to be, totally dissolved."[19] A Committee of Five had been formed to take up the question of independence. Among them was the redheaded gentleman from Monticello who had thought so highly of Paine's work.

When the war for independence broke out months later, Thomas Paine was among the first to volunteer. He served with General Washington's army in New Jersey and earned a place for himself among America's earliest war correspondents by writing a series of dispatches about the war. Among his most famous lines from those dispatches, called *The American Crisis*, was this one: "These are the times that try men's souls. The summer soldier and the sunshine patriot will, in this crisis, shrink from the service of their country; but he that stands it *now*, deserves the love and thanks of man and woman. Tyranny, like hell, is not easily conquered; yet we have this consolation with us, that the harder the conflict, the more glorious the triumph."

December 1776 wasn't the first time Paine had found himself going from a place where things had been to a place where they could be. Much like his journey across the Atlantic years earlier, his journey across the Delaware strengthened his resolve even as it brought about deep personal suffering and privation. Things worth fighting for require sacrifice. The ideas of independence were not yet won. But having captured the minds of the American people, Paine was now fighting to win the war sparked by his own words.

This war was not inevitable. While Paine had inspired the colonies to rebellion, it would take the mind and pen of another individual, with input from a few others, to state clearly and eloquently the grounds on which this rebellious stand was taken. If the Americans could not make a strong moral case, their efforts would cease to be a revolution of ideas and could instead be dismissed as mere colonial unrest. The task of finding the words to elevate their cause for political independence fell, of course, to Thomas Jefferson. And there was a straight and remarkably short line from Paine's *Common Sense* to Jefferson's Declaration of Independence, which would be drafted several months after the pamphlet had lit the fires of independence in the minds of the American colonists—including that of Jefferson. Without the first document, it's not likely the second would have come into being— and certainly not in 1776.

CHAPTER EIGHT

Committee of Five, Genius of One

The committee for drawing the declaration of Independence desired me to do it. It was accordingly done. . . .

—THOMAS JEFFERSON, *AUTOBIOGRAPHY*

WILLIAMSBURG, VIRGINIA
May 15, 1776

SINCE THE CROWN DISBANDED THE HOUSE OF BURGESSES, VIRginians had been governing themselves by convening periodically in Williamsburg. Although these meetings had occurred outside British government sanction, the earlier gatherings had not broached the topic of independence, and delegates even expressed hope for reconciliation with Britain. The delegates to the third convention—held in July 1775 and presided over by Edmund Randolph's uncle Peyton—upon their adjournment "publicly and solemnly declare[d], before God and the world, that we do bear faith and true allegiance to his majesty, George the Third, our only lawful and rightful King," and would "endeavor by every honorable means to promote a restoration of that friendship and amity which so long and happily subsisted between our fellow subjects in Great Britain and the inhabitants of America."[1]

But by the time the Fifth Virginia Convention came to order in May 1776, the situation had changed significantly. In a sign of what was to come, some legislative "old business" was laid to rest before the new business could begin. On May 6, before the convention came to order, forty-five members of the old House of Burgesses gathered. According to their official minutes, "Several Members met, but did neither proceed to Business, nor adjourn, as a House of Burgesses."[2]

Instead, they dissolved the old royally sanctioned colonial legislature for good, because, according to a later report, it was "their opinion that the people could not now be legally represented according to the ancient [British] Constitution, which has been subverted by the King, Lords and Commons of Great Britain."[3] They needed something new—new representation in a system based around guarantees of unalienable rights and supported by the consent of the governed. They may not have known it yet, but they needed the Declaration of Independence.

Though the House of Burgesses had been previously disbanded by Lord Dunmore, it is a testament to the revolutionaries' commitment to self-government that they decided, in the words of one of the attendees, to "let that body die" by their own actions, not those of a royal appointee.[4] They "dissolved themselves accordingly."[5] After the last entry in their minutes, written in "dramatically large letters," was the word *FINIS*.[6] The colonial legislature was gone for good, and full responsibility for representing the people rested on the 112 members of the Virginia Convention, which came to order later that same day.

They came from all corners of the colony, from the Chesapeake Bay coastline to the mountains and valleys beyond the Blue Ridge in what is now West Virginia. Among them were such luminaries as James Madison and Patrick Henry. Hugh Blair Grigsby, a legislator and historian in nineteenth-century Virginia who worked on state business with Madison, reported that "many of the members from the interior had come to the city well armed," in case Lord Dunmore, still lurking off the coast, "might peep in upon them . . . merely to see what they were about."[7]

The people of Williamsburg hovered around the stately brick capitol building "to see what they were about" as well. Blacksmiths and farriers left their forges and stables, merchants left their shops, women arrived with children in hand. Even patrons of the local taverns left food and drink on their tables and wandered out to see what all the excitement was about. The Virginia Convention had been in session for more than a week, and word had spread around town that the delegates were preparing to take an important vote. On the grounds outside the Capitol, the assembled Virginians chatted among themselves as the air itself seemed to crackle with nervous energy.

It was nothing compared with the energy that animated the discussion on the other side of the wall. Inside the capitol building, Edmund Randolph sat at his place in the chamber, taking it all in. At twenty-two, Randolph was the youngest delegate to the Fifth Virginia Convention, the latest in a series of legislative assemblies that had taken place periodically since the summer of 1774, when

Lord Dunmore, Virginia's royal governor, had dissolved the "official" colonial representative body, the House of Burgesses.

The Randolphs were an old and prominent family in the oldest and most prominent British colony in America. Edmund's father, John Randolph, had served as Virginia's attorney general under the royal administration. They were unquestionably members of the Virginia elite, in whose ranks were counted the descendants of the colony's (and North America's) earliest English settlers. They prided themselves on their close ties with the mother country and their status as the "fourth realm" of the British kingdom.

Revolutionary fervor was sweeping the colony, thanks in no small part to Thomas Paine's explosive tract, published several months earlier. Despite this upheaval, Virginia was still technically operating under its official Great Seal, which bore the motto "Behold Virginia the Fourth Realm"—placing the colony on equal footing with the Kingdom's other realms of Britain (England and Scotland), France, and Ireland.[8]

The story of the Randolph family illustrates the personal divisions that were shaking the American colonies in the lead-up to their great political division with Britain. Though young Edmund Randolph was committed to the cause of revolution, his convictions put him at odds with his own parents. Wanting no part of rebellion against the Crown, his parents had returned to England. But Edmund was not the only revolutionary in the family: His uncle Peyton Randolph had embraced the cause as well and took his like-minded nephew under his wing.[9]

In 1775, Edmund Randolph went north to put his life on the line as an officer on George Washington's staff. But his service with the Continental Army was cut short. The sudden death of his uncle Peyton brought him back to Virginia, where, in the spring of 1776, he found himself representing the City of Williamsburg as the capital's delegate to the convention being held there.

Despite his relative youth and political inexperience, Edmund was well aware that this was a critical meeting. The revolutionary activity in Britain's "fourth realm" was reaching a fever pitch. British administration had, in practice, ceased to exist in June 1775 when Lord Dunmore, fearing a rebel attack, had abandoned his office as governor of Virginia and fled to a British warship off the colony's coast. From his floating headquarters he attempted to organize loyalist militia within the colony, but his forces had been handily defeated by the revolutionary Virginians at the Battle of Great Bridge in December. On the first day of 1776, Dunmore's forces burned the port of Norfolk and sailed away.

With the royal governor gone, the Virginians were busy governing themselves, and the business in the early days of the Fifth Convention was fairly routine, though important. The members discussed mostly military matters important to the defense of Virginia against British and loyalist troops.[10] The schedule was grueling, with committee meetings in the early morning, general convention sessions from the late morning into the evening, and more committee meetings late into the night. One delegate wrote: "The committees met at seven, and remained in session until the hour of nine, when the Convention was assembled, which rarely adjourned until five in the afternoon. After dinner and a little refreshment, the committees sit again until nine or ten at night."[11]

After about a week of discussions following this intense timetable—which would give most politicians in today's Washington heart palpitations—the debate turned to the question of independence. By this point, however, there was only so much left to discuss. It was clear to the delegates that their constituents overwhelmingly favored independence from Great Britain. William Aylett, a delegate from King William County, observed that "the people of this Country almost unanimously cry aloud for independence," and the delegates from Cumberland County had been urged by their neighbors to "bid . . . a good night forever" to King George III.[12]

Only one member of the convention voiced opposition to separation from Britain during the two days of debate in Williamsburg. Robert Carter Nicholas, grandson of the extraordinarily wealthy planter Robert "King" Carter, expressed his doubts about the American colonies' ability to go it alone. He was "a victim to conscience," Edmund Randolph explained, "being dubious of the competency of America in so arduous a contest."[13] Nicholas's opposition must have been slightly awkward for the pro-independence Randolph—in just a few months, Randolph was to marry Nicholas's daughter Elizabeth.

Another note of caution was sounded early during the independence debate by a voice that few might have expected: Patrick Henry. Famous for his fiery rhetoric, Henry was in favor of breaking away from Britain, but he thought that perhaps the final blow should be delayed until other world powers, such as France, had been lined up to support the newly independent colonies.[14]

But this was no time for caution. It was a time for action. And Patrick Henry, brilliant politician that he was, knew how to read a crowd. Soon, he was holding forth in his trademark style, and Edmund Randolph was entranced. Though at first Henry spoke dispassionately about independence, "after some time," according to Randolph, "he appeared in an element for which he was born." He was "aroused by the now apparent spirit of the people."

Rooted to his seat, Randolph listened to Henry's profound thunderations: "As a pillar of fire, which, notwithstanding the darkness of the prospect, would conduct to the promised land, he inflamed, and was followed by the convention. His eloquence unlocked the secret spring of the human heart, robbed danger of all its terror, and broke the keystone in the arch of royal power."[15]

The resolution adopted by the convention on May 15 declared that all hope of reconciliation with King George III and his government was dead, since all attempts by colonists to deal amicably with London had, "instead of a redress of grievances . . . produced, from an imperious and vindictive Administration, increased insult, oppression, and a vigorous attempt to effect our total destruction." The Virginians resolved "that the Delegates appointed to represent this Colony in General Congress be instructed to propose to that respectable body to declare the United Colonies free and independent States, absolved from all allegiance to, or dependence upon, the Crown or Parliament of Great Britain." But self-government was a serious business, not to be taken lightly, so at the same time they resolved "to prepare a Declaration of Rights, and such a plan of Government as will be most likely to maintain peace and order in this Colony, and secure substantial and equal liberty to the people."[16]

The resolutions passed unanimously.

As the final vote came down, the crowd outside the Capitol erupted in cheers. "The exultation here was extreme," wrote convention delegate Thomas Ludwell Lee to his brother Richard

Henry Lee at the Continental Congress in Philadelphia.[17] The British flag that flew from the Capitol was immediately hauled down, and in its place was hoisted the Continental Colors. This flag, later known as the Grand Union Flag, featured thirteen white and red stripes with a British Union Jack in the upper left corner. Until the adoption of the Stars and Stripes in 1777, this was independent America's first flag, a symbol of the colonists' respect for the British rights and liberties that they were willing to fight to reclaim from a king who had refused to respect them. If they couldn't claim those rights as British subjects, they would do so as American citizens.

It was official: Virginia's citizens had declared independence. Some three hundred miles to the north, the Continental Congress was prepared to consider that very question on behalf of their fellow Americans. And yet another Virginian would lead the charge.

"SIGN OF THE GOLDEN EAGLE" CABINETRY SHOP, PHILADELPHIA
May 16, 1776

At the moment, all Thomas Jefferson wanted was a mug of water. But to get a mug of water, he would have to get up from his bed. To get up from his bed, he would have to open his eyes. And that was the *last* thing Jefferson wanted to do. If he kept his eyes closed, the headache subsided, if only a little bit.

They seemed to be lessening in intensity, or at least Jefferson hoped they were. He was by now accustomed to these debilitating headaches, which had been plaguing him since the age of nineteen. Now, at the age of thirty-three, he accepted that he could never be sure when they would strike—but when they did, there wasn't much he could do. The latest bout had first hit him about six weeks ago, and he had a good idea what had brought it on. The headaches often had something to do with stress, and at the end of March 1776, Jefferson had experienced one of the most stressful events that could befall a young man in the prime of life. On March 31, his mother, Jane Randolph Jefferson, had suffered a stroke and died.

The physical pain of the headaches compounded Jefferson's grief. They also made him unable to travel, thus delaying his return to Philadelphia to rejoin the Continental Congress. He finally did arrive on May 14, and he proceeded to the cabinetry shop run by Benjamin Randolph under the "Sign of the Golden Eagle" on Chestnut Street. Randolph also rented out rooms on his premises, and Jefferson had stayed there in the past, as had other congressional representatives. While his fellow Virginians in Williamsburg were busy debating independence, Jefferson was settling in in Philadelphia and trying to shake off the residual headache.

His colleagues at the Continental Congress had been busy in his absence as well. On May 10, they passed a resolution that encouraged self-government in each colony and even hinted at the prospect of national, independent self-government. They urged the people of each colony, who had been working under provisional governments since the breakdown of British rule, "to adopt such Government as shall in the Opinion of the Representatives of the People best conduce to the Happiness and Safety of their Constituents in particular, and America in general." This measure was pushed by John Adams and Richard Henry Lee, and Adams later wrote that he considered its passage "a decisive Event."[18]

Five days later, it was decided that this resolution needed an appropriate preamble, which Adams duly supplied. He argued that because "his Britannic Majesty, in conjunction with the Lords and Commons of Great Britain," had stripped his American subject of their rights as his subjects, ignored their pleas for redress, and sent his forces along with foreign mercenaries (including Hessians from King George's family homeland of Germany) to destroy them, "it appears absolutely irreconcileable to reason, and good Conscience, for the People of these Colonies now to take the Oaths and Affirmations necessary for the support of any Government under the Crown of Great Britain."

To that end, Adams declared, "it is necessary that the Exercise of every kind of Authority under the said Crown should be totally suppressed, and all the Powers of Government exerted under the Authority of the People of the Colonies, for the preservation of internal peace, Virtue and good order, as well as for the defence of their Lives, Liberties and Properties against the hostile Invasions and cruel depredations of their Enemies."[19] This, in effect, was John Adams's declaration of independence.

Jefferson recognized its importance as well, and he knew he had to send word back to the Virginians then engaged in their convention. So, on May 16, he roused himself, furrowed his brow against the last vestiges of his headache, and sat down to write a letter to Thomas Nelson, his fellow Virginian, who had left the Continental Congress briefly to attend the convention in Williamsburg.

Jefferson explained that he "arrived here last Tuesday after being detained hence six weeks longer than I intended by a malady" (his headaches). He further noted that matters were made worse by his "uneasy anxious state"—he had wanted to bring his wife, Martha, along with him, but she was pregnant and unable to travel.

He enclosed a copy of the "vote of yesterday on the subject of government," and argued that "in truth it is the whole object of the present controversy; for should a bad government be instituted for us in future it had been as well to have accepted at first the bad one offered to us from beyond the water without the risk and expence of contest."[20] If the colonies weren't able to get the business of self-government right, they might as well have remained under British rule.

He also asked Nelson for news of what was going on at the Virginia Convention. "I suppose they will tell us what to say on the subject of independence," he mused, then remarked that while he was back in Virginia he "took great pains to enquire into the sentiments of the people on that head," or at least the people who lived near him. "In the upper counties," he reported, "I think I may safely say nine out of ten are for it."

Unbeknownst to Jefferson, the Virginia Convention had voted just the day before to instruct their delegates in Philadelphia "what to say on the subject of independence"—they were for it, and ready to establish their own government as well. Furthermore, the person entrusted to carry the official copy of the Virginia Convention's resolution to Philadelphia was none other than Thomas Nelson, who was returning north anyway to retake his seat in Congress.[21] Jefferson's letter likely passed Nelson in transit, but news of the Virginia Convention's resolutions soon reached Philadelphia anyway. The wheels were now in motion. There was no turning back.

GRAFF HOUSE, PHILADELPHIA
June 27

Things were quieter out here, away from the city center. And thank goodness, Thomas Jefferson thought. As he considered his project that had recently drawn to a close, he realized that it would have been difficult to finish had he remained in Benjamin Randolph's furniture shop. Almost as soon as he arrived in Philadelphia, Jefferson had complained: "I think, as the excessive heats of the city are coming on fast, to endeavor to get lodgings in the skirts of the town where I may have the benefit of a freely circulating air."[22]

On the "skirts"—the outskirts—of Philadelphia, at the corner of Seventh and High Streets, he found new lodgings in the home of Jacob Graff. At the time, this was "a more pastoral setting," according to Patrick Glennon of the Historical Society of Pennsylvania.[23] Graff was a brick mason and had recently completed a spacious brick home for himself and his family. Jefferson moved in on May 23. He took quarters on the second floor, which had a bedroom and a separate study in which he could work.[24] Among the personal items he took with him from his first billet was a mahogany lap desk—also known as a "writing box"—which had been designed by Jefferson himself and crafted in Randolph's furniture shop.[25] Such a convenient implement would come in handy in the weeks to come.

The Graffs lived downstairs, but Jefferson was not alone on the upper floors. Living with him was Robert Hemings, a slave who had traveled with him from Monticello. "Hemings," Glennon explains, "likely slept in the garret"—the attic—"of the Graff

House, as was customary for personal slave servants at the time."[26] The work undertaken by Jefferson at the Graff House in June 1776 touched significantly on the slave trade, and it is difficult to avoid speculation on whether the presence of Hemings had any influence on his thought, especially because of an even closer connection between the two men. Hemings also happened to be Jefferson's half-brother-in-law, the son of Martha's father, John Wayles, and an enslaved woman named Elizabeth.

But for the moment, Jefferson was alone in his study. Before him, laid upon his mahogany lap desk, was a sheet of parchment headed: "A Declaration of the Representatives of the UNITED STATES OF AMERICA, in General Congress assembled." Tomorrow, on the twenty-eighth of June, the whole "General Congress assembled" would see this document for the first time, the product of the committee they had directed to draft it more than two weeks before. It was to be presented by the committee, but Jefferson was secure in the knowledge that it was mostly his work.

But it was another Virginian who set the process for its creation by Congress in motion. On June 7, Richard Henry Lee, whose brother Thomas Lee had written so excitedly from the Virginia Convention in Williamsburg, officially acted on the orders that the convention had issued. On behalf of the Virginia delegation and the people of his colony, Lee proposed the resolution that "these United Colonies are, and of right ought to be, free and independent States, that they are absolved from all allegiance to the British Crown, and that all political connection between them and the State of Great Britain is, and ought to be, totally dissolved."[27]

Independence was not to be decided on June 7, 1776, however.

The Continental Congress was still a political body, and political processes still had to play out. Votes had to be counted and lined up, and the definitive stance of each delegation on the independence question ascertained. In order make time to do this, debate on Lee's resolution was postponed until July 1.

This did not mean the question of independence would remain dormant in the intervening weeks. In order to be ready for an eventual separation, Congress appointed a committee on June 11 to begin work on a formal declaration of the colonies' independence from Great Britain. Named to this committee were Jefferson, John Adams, Benjamin Franklin, Robert Livingston of New York, and Roger Sherman of Connecticut.

The story of how exactly Jefferson was chosen to pen the initial draft has been the subject of debate since the early days of the Republic. Jefferson himself stated simply: "The committee for drawing the declaration of Independence desired me to do it."[28] By John Adams's account, however, he was originally slated to work in tandem with Jefferson—"the Committee met," he recalled, "discussed the subject, and then appointed Mr. Jefferson and me to make the draught." Upon meeting with Jefferson shortly thereafter, he states that "Jefferson proposed to me to make the draught."[29] Adams then recounted that he cajoled the younger man to take it upon himself entirely, over Jefferson's objections, by offering three reasons: "You are a Virginian, and Virginia ought to appear at the head of this business . . . I am obnoxious, suspected and unpopular; You are very much otherwise . . . You can write ten times better than I can."[30] Thus, Adams convinced Jefferson to take on the work. But Jefferson, much later in life, disputed this account: "They unanimously pressed on myself alone to undertake the draught," he wrote in 1823.[31]

Whether Jefferson was chosen outright or flattered into the job by Adams, one thing is agreed upon by all accounts: the recognition of Jefferson's skill with the pen. Adams recalled Jefferson's "happy talent at composition," and the "peculiar felicity of expression" in his writing. He already had a reputation as a "renaissance man," and almost exactly a year before had been heavily involved with the drafting of the "Declaration of the Causes and Necessity for Taking Up Arms" on behalf of the Continental Congress.

The drafting of the Declaration was hardly the only piece of congressional business in which Jefferson was engaged at the time. He, like all of his fellow delegates, was kept busy with the work of a number of different committees. Jefferson was assigned to some thirty-four in the period between June 1775 and September 1776 alone.[32] And he was known for throwing himself into all of his committee work. Adams recalled that "though a silent member in Congress, he was so prompt, frank, explicit and decisive upon Committees."[33] We could use more "prompt, frank, explicit and decisive" members on U.S. Senate committees today!

With all of this other business going on, it is estimated that Jefferson spent only two or three days working on his original draft.[34] Then he began an editing process, the details of which are still a source of fascination for historians. The definitive parsing of exactly who changed what in the Declaration draft and when is the subject of Julian Boyd's *The Declaration of Independence: The Evolution of the Text*, first published during World War II. But even Boyd, and the historians who came after him, are unable to say with certainty who was responsible for all of the changes made to Jefferson's draft before it was presented to the full Congress.

The first people to see the draft after Jefferson finished it were Adams and Franklin. Jefferson himself reported this: "I communicated it separately to Dr Franklin and Mr Adams requesting their corrections; because they were the two members of whose judgments and amendments I wished most to have the benefit before presenting it to the Committee."[35] In the original letter to James Madison in which he explained this, the word *separately* was emphasized.

There is some evidence to suggest that though Adams and Franklin reviewed the draft separately, they did so at different times. Adams remembered that he objected to a passage "which called the King a Tyrant . . . for I never believed George to be a tyrant in disposition and in nature; I always believed him to be deceived by his Courtiers on both sides of the Atlantic, and in his Official capacity only, Cruel." Adams was willing to give the benefit of the doubt to George the man, but Adams had no doubt of the cruelty of his acts "in his Official capacity" as King George III, or of those taken by his government. In any event, he declined to change Jefferson's draft at this early stage, because "Franklin and Sherman were to inspect it afterwards."[36] This would support Boyd's theory that "Jefferson presented the Rough Draft to Adams first, who made his copy, and later to Franklin."[37]

During the drafting process, Franklin was dealing with a nasty attack of gout and spent most of his time at home. Fortunately, his home was only a block away from the Graff House.[38] A note from Jefferson to Franklin survives in which Jefferson writes: "The inclosed paper has been read and with some small alterations approved of by the committee. Will Doctr. Franklyn be so good as to peruse it and suggest such alterations as his more enlarged view of the subject will dictate?" This note has been tentatively dated to June 21, 1776, and is thought to have accompanied a version of the Declaration draft.[39] This would track well with a letter Franklin wrote to George Washington on the same day, in which Franklin noted: "I am just recovering from a severe Fit of the Gout, which has kept me from Congress . . . so that I know little of what has passed there, except that a Declaration of Independence is preparing," suggesting that he was involved in the editing process by this stage.[40]

After Franklin and Adams reviewed the draft, it was submitted to the full Committee of Five. Later in life, the principals involved remembered only minor edits being made in these stages before the full congressional review. "I do not now remember that I made or suggested a single alteration," said Adams of his first review, "and I do not remember that Franklin or Sherman criticized any thing" in the committee.[41] Jefferson, for his part, recalled that Franklin's and Adams's "alterations were two or three only, and merely verbal," after which he "reported it to the Committee, and from them, unaltered to Congress."[42] Julian Boyd's estimation is somewhat more precise. He calculates that fifteen edits were made in the first round involving Adams and Franklin only, and a further thirty-two changes in the full committee editing stage—which in practice involved mostly Adams and Franklin again, with little participation from Livingston or Sherman.[43]

But the question of which mind and which hand were responsible for which changes remains speculative in many cases. Even upon analyzing the handwriting and prose style of the original documents, it is difficult to definitively credit most of the individual edits to Adams, to Franklin, or to Jefferson himself. As the primary author, Jefferson certainly revised his own work as it was being drafted, and he even inserted three new grievances during the committee edit phase. But most of the changes were very minor. One of the more interesting was specifically credited to Franklin in a notation in the margin made by Jefferson: Franklin toned down the phrase "deluge us in blood" to the less graphic "destroy us" when referring to attacks by the King's soldiers, for instance.[44]

The most widely recognizable change to the document before its submission to Congress is, perhaps not surprisingly, attributed variously to Jefferson and his two main editors. Jefferson's original draft opened the second paragraph with "We hold these truths to be sacred & undeniable." In the first round of edits, one of the three men changed "sacred and undeniable" to "self-evident." Popular biographies of Jefferson (by Jon Meacham) and of Franklin (by Walter Isaacson) give credit for this change to Franklin. But Boyd offers evidence that could point in any direction: "This famous and altogether felicitous change has been attributed both to Adams and to Jefferson," but the "feeling as it exhibits for precisely the right word is quite Franklinian in character."[45] Then again, according to Boyd, the handwriting in which "self-evident" was written on the original parchment "bears the appearance of being equally Jeffersonian."[46]

Unless some heretofore undiscovered document surfaces in a dusty archive somewhere, we may never know exactly who decided that we hold our founding truths to be "self-evident" rather than "sacred & undeniable." And perhaps that is precisely as it should be. While we rightly celebrate the genius of Jefferson in drafting the Declaration of Independence, it is important to remember that he was not working completely on his own. None of the Founders were. Their strength came from their unity, despite their different backgrounds, skill sets, and points of view. On the issue that mattered most, the cause of liberty, they were united.

When Jefferson woke up on the morning of June 28, 1776, and joined his fellow committee members to present their work to Congress, they were not just presenting the work of Thomas Jefferson with contributions by John Adams and Benjamin Franklin. The document that Jefferson wrote and Adams and Franklin edited was to speak not just in their voices but with the voices of the whole Congress and, ultimately, the whole nation.

Unfortunately, once the document was submitted to Congress, Jefferson would learn how cacophonous so many voices could be.

CHAPTER NINE

Created Equal

Congress cut off about a quarter part of it, as I
expected they would, but they obliterated some of
the best of it . . .

—JOHN ADAMS, 1822

IN HIS ORIGINAL DRAFT OF THE DECLARATION, JEFFERSON
wrapped up his list of grievances against King George III with
a powerful finale, which deserves to be quoted in full, and in its
original form:

> He has waged cruel war against human nature itself, vio-
> lating it's most sacred rights of life & liberty in the persons
> of a distant people who never offended him, captivating &
> carrying them into slavery in another hemisphere, or to incur
> miserable death in their transportation thither. this piratical
> warfare, the opprobrium of **infidel** powers, is the warfare of
> the CHRISTIAN king of Great Britain. determined to keep

open a market where MEN should be bought & sold, he has prostituted his negative for suppressing every legislative attempt to prohibit or to restrain this execrable commerce: and that this assemblage of horrors might want no fact of distinguished die, he is now exciting those very people to rise in arms among us, and to purchase that liberty of which he has deprived them, & murdering the people upon whom he also obtruded them; thus paying off former crimes committed against the **liberties** of one people, with crimes which he urges them to commit against the **lives** of another.[1]

That "cruel war against human nature itself" was, of course, the African slave trade. Jefferson sought to list this among King George's wrongdoings, in language that asserted the humanity of enslaved people and stood up for their rights, despite their not being remotely represented in the Continental Congress.

Jefferson was a product of and a participant in the slave system. He owned slaves himself and even traveled to Philadelphia with the aforementioned Robert Hemings, his enslaved half-brother-in-law. But this screed against the slave trade was not the first time Jefferson had taken a stand against at least some aspects of the slave system. He records in his memoirs that in his early political career, as a young member of the Virginia House of Burgesses, he "made one effort in that body for the permission of the emancipation of slaves, which was rejected." "Indeed," he grumbled, "during the regal government, nothing liberal could expect success."[2] Thus, in the original Declaration, he made sure to call out the King for "suppressing every legislative attempt to prohibit or to restrain this execrable commerce."

This passage also marked some of the most overtly religious language in Jefferson's original draft. Though "the laws of nature and of nature's god" were invoked by Jefferson's hand, reconciling Enlightenment and religious thinking, the phrase "endowed by their Creator" was not present in the first draft but added later. Jefferson originally stated that our rights were a result of our "equal creation" without mentioning the Creator Himself. But when he contrasted the "infidel powers"—an apparent reference to Muslim slave traders from the Middle East and North Africa—with "the Christian King of Great Britain" he argued in no uncertain terms that the slave trade was not only unwelcome in North America but against the Christian God, who had created not only the slave trader but also the King and the slave.

The editing contributions made by the whole Congress to the work of Jefferson and the Committee of Five should not be discounted. Indeed, Boyd argues, "it is difficult to point out a passage in the Declaration, great as it was, that was not improved by their attention," citing the involvement of such "keen minds" as James Wilson of Pennsylvania and John Witherspoon of New Jersey.[3] There is certainly a case to be made that, rhetorically, sections of Jefferson's wording benefited from the streamlining efforts of his colleagues, which produced some of the memorable phrasing that is known around the world today.

But Julian Boyd, though a preeminent Jefferson scholar, originally wrote his analysis in 1943, and changing times can bend the arc of consideration of the Declaration's editing stage back toward the position staked out early on by Adams—that "some of the best of it" had been removed. This impassioned argument against the slave trade remains a painful reminder of a tragic missed opportunity.

Even at the time, however, John Adams knew that portion wouldn't last. When he first read Jefferson's draft at a meeting of the Committee of Five, he commended "the flights of Oratory with which it abounded, especially that concerning Negro Slavery," a clause "which though I knew his Southern Bretheren would never suffer to pass in Congress, I certainly never would oppose."[4] Jefferson himself also blamed his Southern colleagues for striking out the antislavery language: "The clause . . . reprobating the enslaving [of] the inhabitants of Africa, was struck out in complaisance to South Carolina and Georgia, who had never attempted to restrain the importation of slaves, and who on the contrary still wished to continue it." But the Northern delegates did not get a pass in Jefferson's final judgment: "Our northern brethren also I believe felt a little tender under those censures; for though their people have very few slaves themselves yet they had been pretty considerable carriers of them to others."[5]

But how does this effort to strike a blow against the slave system with the Declaration, and the evident bitterness when that effort failed, factor into Thomas Jefferson's overall legacy on the issue of slavery? This is a question that is still being debated and no doubt will be for decades to come. Numerous people were enslaved by Thomas Jefferson to work his land. His relationship with one of them, Sally Hemings, has been well studied. His view of people of color in general was certainly not especially enlightened, and even in the draft passage denouncing the slave trade he argued they have been "obtruded"—imposed—onto the white colonists by the King's voracious economic appetite. This was a rhetorical stretch to say the least. Nobody was "obtruding" enslaved workers onto Jefferson at Monticello—nobody was *forcing* him to keep them in bondage.

Dr. William Rasmussen of the Virginia Historical Society writes that "Jefferson's relationship with slavery was torturous as he wrestled with this evil for all of his adult life."[6] His efforts to dilute its effect continued well after his work on the Declaration—as a member of Congress in 1784 he was narrowly defeated in an effort to keep slavery out of new states admitted to the Union.[7]

That failure came back to haunt him in 1820 during the debate over whether Missouri should enter the Union as a free or slave state. "This momentous question, like a fire bell in the night, awakened and filled me with terror," Jefferson wrote then. "We have the wolf by the ear," he said of the slavery question, "and we can neither hold him, nor safely let him go. Justice is in one scale, and self-preservation in the other." With his talk of "self-preservation," Jefferson was expressing his fear that black people, if freed from slavery, would turn on the whites who had oppressed them for so long, because the slave system had continued unchecked. He saw the free state versus slave state debate as "the knell of the Union," and tragically observed: "I regret that I am now to die in the belief that the useless sacrifice of themselves, by the generation of '76, to acquire self government and happiness to their country, is to be thrown away by the unwise and unworthy passions of their sons, and that my only consolation is to be that I live not to weep over it."[8]

The Union did not dissolve in Jefferson's lifetime, but the slavery question did indeed tear it asunder a few decades later. In the midst of the Civil War, Abraham Lincoln invoked Jefferson's words at Gettysburg, reflecting that our nation was "conceived in liberty, and dedicated to the proposition that all men are created equal," and that this war was "testing whether that nation, or any nation so conceived, and so dedicated, can long endure."

It has endured, and it will continue to do so as long as we remain dedicated to its founding principles. One American who understood that was Frederick Douglass, who had experienced the worst of America as a slave before claiming his God-given freedom and becoming a leading abolitionist. Asked to give a Fourth of July speech in 1852, he delivered a surprising assessment to his largely white audience. "What have I," he asked, "or those I represent, to do with your national independence? Are the great principles of political freedom and of natural justice, embodied in that Declaration of Independence, extended to us?" His answer, of course, was no, and he proclaimed: "This Fourth [of] July is yours, not mine. You may rejoice, I must mourn."[9]

But despite all that, Douglass felt that the simple truths in the Declaration of Independence would be the tools with which true freedom would be eventually extended to all. Later in the speech, he called the Declaration "the ring-bolt to the chain of your nation's destiny." "The principles contained in that instrument are saving principles," he said. "Stand by those principles, be true to them on all occasions, in all places, against all foes, and at whatever cost."

He ended with a powerful prediction that days of slavery in America were numbered. "While drawing encouragement from the Declaration of Independence, the great principles it contains, and the genius of American Institutions, my spirit is also cheered by the obvious tendencies of the age."[10] Douglass expressed his confidence that the timeless principles of the Declaration, solidly grounding the technological and cultural advances brought about by American ingenuity and changing times, would clear the path to freedom.

And so they did, but it took time. In some ways, this is reminiscent of the simple prayer popularly attributed to St. Augustine: "God, make me good, but not yet." As St. Augustine understood that individual humans need time to develop into more moral and better—but never perfect—versions of themselves, so perhaps Jefferson understood that American society needed time to shed the immoral fetters of slavery. By attempting to mitigate the slave trade in the original Declaration, Jefferson expressed a will to start the process earlier than it would have otherwise.

And yet, there remains an undeniable tension between what the Founders believed and the way they lived. Modern minds remain boggled by the fact that Jefferson could write about the equal rights of man while his fellow human beings—wholly owned by himself and his family—worked without pay back at Monticello. Think what a shining example Jefferson might have set had he freed his slaves—or even if, upon his death, he had made provisions for their eventual freedom, as Washington did. He would have shown the superiority of the moral argument against slavery over the soulless economic argument in favor of it. Instead, the tension between moral and economic forces increased over nearly another century before they exploded into bloody war. Had more of our society been guided by conscience rather than by profit, perhaps the slave system would have been abolished earlier and the Civil War avoided.

But sometimes the generation that sparks a monumental change will not be the one to carry it out. Change sometimes depends upon generations that come after. Courage is required in the moment, however, to set the course that other generations can follow to eventually fulfill their promise. By expressing his disapprobation of the slave trade, and enshrining what Frederick

Douglass called the "saving principles" of our society in the Declaration of Independence, Jefferson set that course for future generations of Americans.

Before the new nation could continue on this course, however, it had to fight to keep from being reabsorbed into the British Empire. Across the Atlantic Ocean, His Majesty King George III was incensed at his subjects' disloyalty to the Crown and personal insult to himself. He was not about to lose his American colonies without a fight.

CHAPTER TEN
King George's Call to Arms

No people ever enjoyed more Happiness, or lived under a milder Government, than those now revolted Provinces.

—KING GEORGE III TO PARLIAMENT, OCTOBER 31, 1776

LONDON
October 31, 1776

SIR FRANCIS MOLYNEUX STRODE WITH PURPOSE, HIS FOOTsteps echoing in the cold, empty halls of the Palace of Westminster. He was the seventh of the Molyneux Baronets, a gentleman of the English aristocracy, a loyal courtier to his sovereign—and today he was fulfilling one of his most important duties. In his right hand, balanced on his shoulder, he carried a simple stick of dark ebony wood tipped with gold at both ends. This unique instrument gave Sir Francis his most impressive title—the "Gentleman Usher of the Black Rod," or simply "Black Rod" for short.

There had been a Black Rod serving the British Parliament going all the way back to the fourteenth century. Normally, his duties required him to maintain order and security in the House of Lords, Parliament's upper chamber, where the scions of Britain's oldest families and bearers of its most ancient titles held forth on the day's most pressing issues. Today, however, he was carrying an important formal message to the lower house, the House of Commons, whose members were elected by the people.

As Sir Francis drew closer to the House of Commons chamber, the doors were suddenly slammed shut. But Sir Francis did not break his stride. This was all part of the plan and had been for more than a hundred years. He walked up to the heavy oak doors, raised his rod, and banged deliberately three times.

"Who's there?" called a voice from within.

"Black Rod," Sir Francis answered clearly.

At this, the doors were opened and Sir Francis took his first measured steps into the chamber. Arrayed before him in their tiered benches on either side were the British people's representatives in government, presided over by their Speaker, Fletcher Norton. But the house where the people's voice was supposed to ring loudest was about to get a reminder of where the real power resided.

Sir Francis bowed and made the traditional announcement: "Mr. Speaker, the King commands this honorable House to attend His Majesty immediately in the House of Lords."

It was the opening day of the third session of the Fourteenth Parliament of Great Britain, and as usual, the centerpiece of the day was to be the speech made by the sovereign. The ruler formally known as "His Majesty George the Third, by the grace of God, of Great-Britain, France, and Ireland, King, Defender of the Faith" had already arrived, and taken his place on the throne set up in the chamber of the House of Lords. It had been the task of Sir Francis Molyneux and his black rod to formally invite—or "command"—the Members of Parliament in the House of Commons to make their way to the upper chamber and listen to the speech from the throne along with their noble colleagues.

The activities of the day had so far followed the tradition and protocol so much a feature of British parliamentary rule—then and now. But thanks to unprecedented events thousands of miles away, this was going to be a king's speech unlike any other.

King George III took the throne in 1760, at the tender age of twenty-two, and that same year he commissioned the grand State Coach, which, drawn by eight horses, carried him that October day to the Palace of Westminster to open his Parliament. Now known as the Gold State Coach and still in use in Britain, the carriage drips with gilded carvings, all of which are loaded with symbolism meant to project the divine right and power of the British monarchy. There are lions, the national symbol; there are cherubs, signifying the monarch's rule by God's grace; but perhaps most prominently placed, looming over each wheel, are four figures of Triton.

Triton is a Greek water deity, and his inclusion is meant to symbolize the reach of Britain's—and thus, the King's—power across the seas. A formidable naval power, Britain was said, in the lyrics of a song that had been popular for decades, to "rule the waves" and thereby keep its far-flung colonies around the world in check.

One of those far-flung colonies, however, was in the midst of showing just how wide a gulf, greater even than the sprawling ocean between them, had developed between King George and some of the people he ruled. Three months earlier, English colonists in eastern North America had formally broken away from Great Britain and established themselves no longer as subjects of the Crown but as citizens of the "free and independent states" in which they lived.

In doing so, they claimed to be asserting their rights as Englishmen to enjoy "life, liberty and the pursuit of happiness" to the same degree as their cousins in mainland Britain. Why, they reasoned, should an Englishman living in Boston be subjected to greater rules, regulations, taxes—and perhaps worst of all, the presence of armed soldiers on his streets—when these would have been considered outrageous to any Englishman in London?

It was no small irony that the idea of individual rights and liberties had been present in English government for some time, going back to the Magna Carta of 1215. An assertion of resistance to royal despotism was even built into the very ceremony over which George III was presiding today.

When the doors of the House of Commons had been shut in the face of Black Rod, the messenger of the King, and the nobility, it was a symbolic act of highlighting the independence of the people's elected representatives who met in that chamber. Its roots went back to an incident in 1642 when King Charles I, in the lead-up to the English Civil War, barged into the House of Commons chamber intending to arrest a group of rebellious members led by John Hampden. Such an attack on duly elected Members of Parliament was unconscionable, even by a monarch who ruled by supposed divine right. Hostilities began shortly thereafter, and in 1649 Charles I ended up losing not just his crown but his head.

While the House of Commons retained this flourish of symbolic defiance, they still would admit Black Rod, and they still would rise from their seats to walk to the House of Lords chamber to hear their sovereign speak. The opening of Parliament on October 31, 1776, was no exception. But much of their talk of late was about the rebellious colonists in America who instead of temporarily shutting out the symbols of the monarch's rule were apparently casting them off for good.

Their Declaration of Independence, the document by which the colonists had officially separated themselves from Great Britain, had been issued on July 4 in Philadelphia. In the next few days, word of this dramatic action had apparently reached General William Howe, the commander of British forces in New York. When from his base at Staten Island he dashed off the next dispatches to London, dated July 7 and 8, he focused on reporting troop movements but included this offhand note: "Several Men have within these last two Days come over to this Island . . . and I am informed that the Continental Congress have declared the United Colonies free and independent States."[1]

Howe's letter was published in the *London Gazette* on August 10, marking the first official announcement of the Americans' separation. By the following week, the full Declaration had been printed in the British press and the word was out far and wide.

One of the Members of Parliament now on his way to hear the King speak had had a particularly strong reaction when he heard what had transpired in Philadelphia in July. Edmund Burke, who was then representing the City of Bristol in the House of Commons, had long been one of the voices in support of the American colonists, urging the King and the prime minister, Lord North, to treat them with a spirit of respect and reconciliation. The previous year, Burke stated in the House that "in this character of the Americans, a love of freedom is the predominating feature which marks and distinguishes the whole," but that the "colonies become suspicious, restive, and untractable, whenever they see the least attempt to wrest from them by force" this freedom, which Burke noted was to the Americans "the only advantage worth living for."[2]

Burke understood the Americans, and he had hoped for them to remain subjects of the Crown, but with the full panoply of rights enjoyed by other Englishmen. Now, however, the moment he had dreaded had come to pass. Burke said later that he was "sick at heart" when he heard about the Declaration of Independence. The news "struck [him] to the soul," and he saw there was no hope of reconciliation, no hope of turning back.[3]

Perhaps Burke understood this immediately, and he was not the only parliamentarian who was convinced it was time to simply bid farewell to the American colonies and stop spilling British blood and treasure in a long war in which the colonies enjoyed an obvious home-field advantage. His sovereign, however, felt different, as he would soon reveal.

The members of the House of Commons made their way to the House of Lords chamber to join the noble Peers of the Realm and bishops composing the upper house. The nobles were dressed in brilliant red robes trimmed with ermine, the bishops in simple black and white. And in the center, seated on his throne, sat the man whose presence commanded theirs: King George III.

Not yet forty, the King nonetheless now had nearly two decades of experience on the throne. The crisis in America was, however, proving a difficult one to address. And His Majesty was taking it personally. George III was the first of his royal dynasty—called the Hanoverians, after the family's original seat in Germany—to rule Britain after having actually been born there. His two immediate predecessors, George I and George II, had been born in Germany. But *this* George had been born in London, and he took his identity as an Englishman very seriously. When he first took the throne and made the customary speech to Parliament, into the ghostwritten remarks he added this sentence of his own: "Born and educated in this country, I glory in the name of Britain."[4] Now some rebels sought to rip apart the Britain he held so dear, to tear away a major component of the empire over which he ruled and in whose name he gloried. It was not just his power that these Americans sought to attack—it was his very identity.

And yet, as the monarch sat in Parliament surveying his captive audience, these emotions were kept below the surface. His full—some might even say pudgy—face remained placid, betraying little emotion and giving away no hints as to his mood. George III had made no public pronouncements since news of the Declaration broke in England, and the lords and elected officials assembled waited to hear how he intended to address it.

From the beginning of his speech, his agenda was clear:

"My Lords and Gentlemen," he began, "Nothing could have afforded Me so much Satisfaction as to have been able to inform you, at the Opening of this Session, that the Troubles, which have so long distracted My Colonies in North America, were at an End." He condescended to add his wish that "My unhappy People, recovered from their Delusion, had delivered themselves from the Oppression of their Leaders, and returned to their Duty."[5]

This was an especially awkward start. Not only were the troubles not at an end, they had gotten far worse. But the King swiftly acknowledged this: "So daring and desperate is the Spirit of those Leaders," he said, "whose Object has always been Dominion and Power, that they have now openly renounced all Allegiance to the Crown, and all political Connection with this Country."

His Majesty was almost directly parroting the language of the Declaration itself, as crafted by Thomas Jefferson, which declared that the colonies are "absolved from all Allegiance to the British Crown, and that all political connection between them and the State of Great Britain, is and ought to be totally dissolved."

The King further snarled that the colonists had "rejected, with Circumstances of Indignity and Insult," Britain's attempts at reconciliation—which in the colonists' view had come too little, too late—"and have presumed to set up their rebellious Confederacies for Independent States." He knew this disrespect could not stand and that the entire European colonial system could be in jeopardy if it went unanswered: "If their Treason be suffered to take Root, much Mischief must grow from it, to the Safety of My loyal Colonies, to the Commerce of My Kingdoms, and indeed to the present System of all Europe."

He then called for "unanimity at home" in the cause of pursuing the American war, perhaps anticipating that this latest development would put even more British politicians in the mind of Burke and let the Americans get away with it. To that end, he proceeded to give an update on British victories on the battlefield in New York, make assurances that the other European monarchs were behind him, and remind members of the House of Commons of their duty to fully fund his campaigns.

The King concluded with the opinion that "no people ever enjoyed more Happiness, or lived under a milder Government, than those now revolted Provinces." "My Desire," his final sentence proclaimed, "is to restore to them the Blessings of Law and Liberty, equally enjoyed by every British Subject, which they have fatally and desperately exchanged for all the Calamities of War, and the arbitrary Tyranny of their Chiefs."

His Majesty had saved the most disingenuous claims for last.

The government he claimed was "mild" had in fact visited great oppression, even violence, on the people of those "revolted provinces." They had been taxed into oblivion, bullied by soldiers in the streets of their hometowns, and had their representative assemblies disbanded. Thomas Jefferson had taken great care to detail these and other offenses in the list of grievances against George III, which made up the bulk of his Declaration.

Jefferson and his compatriots had indeed sought "the Blessings of Law and Liberty," but the simple fact was they were *not* "enjoyed equally by every British subject." The British subjects in America were not guaranteed these blessings under the Crown anymore, so they set off to claim them for themselves. That the King still, after their formal split, dismissed this as a "delusion" and sought to bring the Americans to heel showed how out of touch he and his government remained, exhibiting the same lack of understanding that brought this situation into being.

Edmund Burke's first reaction when he heard the news of the Declaration was accurate. Nothing like the Declaration of Independence had been issued before as the foundation for a new nation. The map had been redrawn, the shape of the world had changed—there was no turning back.

LONDON
September 1775

There was a time when there was hope. There was a time when some of the leaders among the American colonists still felt that if they could make their case to the King, if His Majesty could read their words for himself rather than relying on the reports of his scheming ministers and advisers, he would see reason and loosen his stranglehold on their colonies. Further fighting like what had scorched Massachusetts, from Lexington to Concord to Bunker Hill, in the spring and into the summer of 1775 could perhaps be avoided. In September of that year, those hopes rested in the hands of two men: Arthur Lee and Richard Penn. They were charged with delivering a petition addressed "To the King's most excellent Majesty" from his "faithful subjects," the members of the Continental Congress.

The men who shared this mission also shared some aspects of their background: Both came from the ranks of the colonial elite, and both had been educated in England. But in the current conflict between the colonies and the Crown, they had taken different sides.

Richard Penn was the grandson of William Penn, founder of Pennsylvania, and had previously served in the royal administration as lieutenant governor and later acting governor of that colony. A loyalist, he decamped for England when Philadelphia became a center of revolutionary activity, but he agreed to assist the Continental Congress in taking their case to the King.

Arthur Lee, on the other hand, came from that large and active Virginia family that had thrown its considerable resources behind the patriot cause. Two of Arthur's brothers, Richard Henry Lee and Francis Lightfoot Lee, were members of the Congress who had approved the document for which Arthur was now responsible. For him, this mission was not just a political errand but a family matter as well.

The petition borne by Penn and Lee may have been approved by the entire Continental Congress and signed by many of its delegates, but it was largely the brainchild of one man: John Dickinson of Pennsylvania. Dickinson was a leading moderate in the Congress, and in the summer of 1775, as Thomas Jefferson noted, "still retained the hope of reconciliation with the mother country."[6] In the first days of July 1775, Dickinson and Jefferson wrangled over the "Declaration of the Causes and Necessity of Taking Up Arms" against the King's forces, which Congress passed on July 6 of that year. In what Jefferson saw as a consolation prize for Dickinson, Congress allowed him to draw up a second and more conciliatory document addressed directly to King George. It became known as the Olive Branch Petition.

Its tone was almost servile. Greeting the King as "Most Gracious Sovereign," it begged to "entreat your Majesty's gracious attention to this our humble petition." It blamed government officials in London, not the King himself, for the present difficulties, but opted to "decline the ungrateful task of describing the irksome variety of artifices, practiced by many of your Majesty's Ministers," presumably to avoid offending the monarch's delicate ear. Still, Dickinson noted, these ministers "have compelled us to arm in our own defense, and have engaged us in a controversy so peculiarly abhorrent to the affections of your still faithful colonists." Then he really laid it on thick:

> Attached to your Majesty's person, family, and government, with all devotion that principle and affection can inspire, connected with Great Britain by the strongest ties that can unite societies, and deploring every event that tends in any degree to weaken them, we solemnly assure your Majesty, that we not only most ardently desire the former harmony between her and these colonies may be restored . . .

He concluded by asking the King to intervene more directly in colonial affairs, "that your royal authority and influence may be graciously interposed to procure us relief from our afflicting fears and jealousies."[7]

Jefferson, for one, was appalled—and his memoirs suggest that he wasn't the only one. "The disgust against this humility was general," he said, "and Mr. Dickinson's delight at its passage was the only circumstance which reconciled them to it." Jefferson felt the whole exercise was a waste of time, "a signal proof of [Congress's] indulgence to Mr. Dickinson." Yet Dickinson's colleagues approved the document on July 8, 1775.

Jefferson could not help but recount an awkward incident following the petition's passage when, despite the debate being closed, Dickinson "could not refrain from rising and expressing his satisfaction" in an impromptu speech.

"There is but one word, Mr. President, in the paper which I disapprove," he said in conclusion, "and that is the word 'Congress.'"

At this, Jefferson's fellow Virginian Benjamin Harrison rose and responded: "There is but one word in the paper, Mr. President, of which I approve, and that is the word 'Congress.'"[8]

By late August, the petition—bearing the signatures of Jefferson and Harrison among those of their fellow delegates, despite their objections—was in the hands of Richard Penn and Arthur Lee in London. They sent a copy to Lord Dartmouth, secretary of state for the colonies, for his advance review and requested a meeting to formally present him with the original. Seeking to bolster their case, Lee also wrote to Edmund Burke, whose sympathy for the colonial cause was well known, inviting him to join them for the meeting with Dartmouth.

Burke politely declined, but he wrote to Lee to express his support for the Congress's petition. "I am convinced," he remarked, perhaps overly optimistically, "that nothing is further from the desires of the gentlemen who compose it, than to separate themselves from their allegiance to their sovereign, or their subordinate connection with their mother country." Rather, Burke suggested,

"I believe they sincerely wish for an end of these unhappy troubles, in which, while all are distressed, they must be the first and greatest sufferers."[9]

Burke's words echoed in Arthur Lee's memory as he and Penn waited to be shown into Lord Dartmouth's office in London on September 2, 1775. The day before, they had finally presented him with the original petition, which he had promised to bring to the King himself. Now the two colonial agents were anxious for His Majesty's answer. But when Lord Dartmouth arrived, his news was surprising. "As His Majesty did not receive it on the throne," His Lordship reported, "no answer would be given."[10]

Lee was aghast. If the fighting continued, soon it would stretch from New England down to his native Virginia. But he had found Dartmouth to be "a man of great candor and amiableness of character," so he felt free to speak his peace. He gave the only response that came to him.

"I am sorry," he told Dartmouth, "that his majesty has adopted a measure which will occasion so much bloodshed."

But Dartmouth was dismissive. "If I thought it would be the cause of shedding one drop of blood I should never have concurred in it," he replied. "But I cannot be of an opinion that it will be attended by any such consequences."

Lee would not back down. "My lord," he continued firmly, "as sure as we exist, this answer will be the cause of much blood being shed in America, and of most dreadful consequences."[11]

With that, Lee and Penn excused themselves. They had to dash off a quick report of their meeting so it could make it across the Atlantic as quickly as possible. They left Dartmouth with that dire prediction ringing in the air.

They were right, of course. The consequences would be dreadful. Not least because King George had already made up his mind before the petition was even submitted: The rebels in America were not to be compromised with; they were to be crushed.

On August 23, as Penn and Lee were preparing for their meeting with Dartmouth, King George III issued a royal proclamation. His American subjects, it observed, "misled by dangerous and ill designing men, and forgetting the allegiance which they owe to the power that has protected and supported them," had "at length proceeded to open and avowed rebellion." His Majesty accused them of "traitorously preparing, ordering and levying war against us," and commanded that "all our Officers, civil and military, are obliged to exert their utmost endeavours to suppress such rebellion, and to bring the traitors to justice."[12]

The King had decided that the time for compromise was over, and as such he was in no mood to receive the petition brought to him just days later. In the following weeks, he addressed Parliament and stated his resolve even more clearly. The colonists, he was convinced, were trying to break away, and His Majesty simply would not permit it:

"The rebellious war now levied is become more general," he observed on October 27, 1775, "and is manifestly carried on for the purpose of establishing an independent empire." King George was preparing for American independence well before the Declaration was issued. He viewed this as an affront to British identity—to *his* identity:

The object is too important, the spirit of the British nation too high, the resources with which God hath blessed her too numerous, to give up so many colonists which she has planted with great industry, nursed with great tenderness, encouraged with many commercial advantages, and protected and defended at much expence of blood and treasure.[13]

To keep his empire together, King George III knew that more "blood and treasure" would be the answer.

CHAPTER ELEVEN

"America Is Lost!"

The present accounts from America seem to put a
final stop to all negotiation. Farther concession is
a joke.

—KING GEORGE III TO LORD NORTH, AUGUST 12, 1778

LONDON
January 31, 1778

IT WAS NEARLY HALF PAST ONE IN THE AFTERNOON WHEN KING
George III sat down to compose a note to his prime minister,
Lord North. More than two years of war in the American colonies
had taken their toll on Great Britain—its soldiers were dying,
money was flying out of the royal treasury, and yet the rebellious
colonists still had not been brought to heel. In July 1776, they
formally declared their so-called independence, as King George
had predicted the previous fall. More recently, on October 17,

1777, his army had suffered a significant defeat at Saratoga in New York when British general John Burgoyne, surrounded by a superior force, surrendered his army of thousands to American general Horatio Gates.

Hardly anyone had thought the ragtag American troops capable of such a large-scale victory. The British were stunned. Even more significantly, the French, who had been weighing whether or not to formally support the American cause against their traditional British enemies, were impressed.

Though this was a setback, no doubt, it so distressed King George that by the beginning of the year 1778, his own prime minister was beginning to entertain the idea of negotiating a peace settlement with the American rebel leaders. Now was not the time for his top government official to go wobbly. His Majesty decided that Lord North's spine needed straightening and wrote to him to stiffen his resolve:

> You will remember that before the recess I strongly advised you not to bind yourself to bring forward a proposition for restoring tranquility to North America, not from any absurd ideas of unconditional submission my mind never harboured, but from perceiving that whatever can be proposed will be liable not to bring America back to a sense of attachment to the mother country, yet to dissatisfy this country, which has in the most handsome manner cheerfully carried on the contest, and therefore has a right to have the struggle continued until convinced that it is in vain.[1]

His Majesty's account of the situation, however, had a few serious gaps with reality. Samuel B. Griffith II, a decorated U.S. Marine officer in World War II who became a military historian in later life, points out that George III's line about "absurd ideas of unconditional submission" is in fact "a falsehood," as His Majesty "had for years insisted on unconditional submission" by the Americans.[2]

The King may have been attempting to soothe Lord North's anxieties and present his own views as less hard-line than they really were. As a matter of fact, while George III himself may have "in the most handsome manner cheerfully carried on the contest," the same could not be said for his prime minister. Lord North was anything but cheerful. Indeed, historian Andrew O'Shaughnessy points out that by this point he "lacked conviction in the cause and was increasingly despondent," while King George was "more than simply committed to the cause, but became the chief driving force in the war for America."[3]

But events over the next few days would change the situation, and with it, His Majesty's tune.

February 9

The British spy network, the precursor to today's MI-6, had been hard at work. King George was able to report to Lord North that the latest intelligence, "if certain, shows the veil will soon be drawn off by the Court of France"—meaning France would openly declare an alliance with the Americans against Great Britain.[4]

The French threat was enough to get George III to take the idea of peace terms seriously, and while he had held back Lord

North from pursing that goal little more than a week prior, he now cajoled his prime minister. This news, he wrote, "makes me wish you would not delay bringing your American proposition . . . into the House of Commons."[5]

But though King George entertained ideas of peace, his mind remained firmly fixed on war, which he intended to micromanage even if the French entered the fray:

> . . . should a French war be our fate, I trust you will concur with me in the only means of making it successful, the withdrawing of the greatest part of them [the troops] from America, and employing them against the French and Spanish settlements . . .[6]

He further explained that "if we are to be carrying on a land-war against the rebels and against these two powers," their efforts would "be feeble in all parts and consequently unsuccessful." He was prepared to make the American rebellion into a war between European powers.

March 13

It had been a tumultuous day for the government. The French had made their move. The Marquis de Noailles, King Louis XVI's ambassador in London, formally informed the secretary of state, Lord Weymouth, that "a treaty of friendship and commerce" had been signed between King Louis and "the United States of North America, who are in full possession of independence, as pronounced by them on the fourth of July, 1776."

It was nearly eleven at night before King George III had time to communicate his thoughts to Lord North. As the candelabra flickered on his desk, he scratched out his observation that "the paper delivered this day by the French Ambassador is certainly equivalent to a declaration." His mind raced as he sketched out new ideas for the positioning of his forces across the ocean:

> [W]hat occurs now is to fix what numbers are necessary to defend New York, Rhode Island, Nova Scotia, and the Floridas: it is a joke to think of keeping Pennsylvania, for we must from the army now in America form a corps sufficient to attack the French islands, and two or three thousand men ought to be employed with the fleet to destroy the ports and wharves of the rebels.[7]

Now that the French were firmly in the fight, King George was determined to direct a two-front war after all. But Lord North, still contemplating the prospect of peace, had other ideas.

August 12

Just three days after the French openly declared support for the American cause, Parliament approved a peace commission to travel to America and negotiate with the American government to bring the war to a close. Headed by Frederick Howard, the fifth Earl of Carlisle, the group set out in April with King George's reluctant approval.

Their mission, simply put, was a failure. According to Robert

McNamee of Oxford University, "the Commissioners clearly tried to stir anti-Congressional feelings in the colonists"—one commissioner was accused of bribery, and Carlisle himself was challenged to a duel by none other than the Marquis de Lafayette after directing some undiplomatic comments toward the French.[8] General George Washington, encamped with the Continental Army, observed in a letter that "the Enemy are beginning to play a game, more dangerous than their efforts by arms . . . which threatens a fatal blow to American independence, and to her liberties of course: They are endeavouring to ensnare the people by specious allurements of peace."[9]

The Continental Congress would accept no offer of peace without Britain's recognition of their independence, which was, of course, a nonstarter for the royal commissioners. In their official rejection letter, the Congress pointed out that the Carlisle Commission's terms "suppose the people of these states to be subjects of the crown of Great Britain, and are founded on an idea of dependence, which is utterly inadmissible."[10]

This rejection was issued July 17, and the news had reached England by August 12, when King George, perhaps feeling vindicated by the failure of a peace settlement, bluntly declared to Lord North: "The present accounts from America seem to put a final stop to all negotiation. Farther concession is a joke."[11]

"We must content ourselves with distressing the rebels," the King wrote to his prime minister from Windsor Castle, "and not think of any other conduct till the end of the French [war], which, if successful, will oblige the rebels to submit to more reasonable [terms] than can at this hour be obtained."[12]

War was still the answer. War and war alone would bring the American colonists back into the empire's fold.

At least, that's what King George hoped.

ST. JAMES'S PALACE, LONDON
June 1, 1785

The door shut, leaving only three men in the room. Standing just inside the door, having just entered, was John Adams, the first-ever U.S. ambassador to the Court of St. James. Standing politely behind Adams, having just shown him in, was Francis Godolphin Osborne, Marquess of Carmarthen, Great Britain's secretary of state for foreign affairs. In front of them stood His Majesty King George III.

The King and the ambassador looked at each other for a moment. Ten years before, John Adams had been officially a subject of the man who stood before him. Then Adams had joined a rebellion in defiance of his sovereign. That rebellion had turned into a war to secure independence for a new nation, a nation it was now Adams's charge to represent. The war between Great Britain and her American colonies—now the United States of America—had ended two years before, and Adams's visit was to play a critical part in mending the transatlantic relationship.

Adams could have no way of knowing how deeply this meeting affected the man before him. Even in 1780, King George wrote, "I can never suppose this country so far lost to all ideas of self-importance as to be willing to grant America independence."[13] Two years later, peace negotiations were being conducted with the Americans.

In March 1782, King George III drafted, but ultimately never delivered, what would have been a truly remarkable speech. "A long Experience and a serious attention to the Strange Events that have successively arisen," he wrote, "has gradually prepared My mind to expect the time when I should be no longer of Utility to this Empire; that hour is now come; I am therefore resolved to resign My Crown."[14] He was prepared to abdicate over the loss of the American colonies. The American Revolution not only toppled King George from dominance over eastern North America; it very nearly toppled him altogether.

And yet he chose to remain on the throne and gradually started to consider how an independent America would fit into his world. At some point in the 1780s, he sketched out some notes based on an essay by the agricultural scientist Arthur Young.[15] "America is lost!" it began. "Must we fall beneath the blow? Or have we resources that may repair the mischief?" These notes discussed "mischief" largely of an economic nature, lamenting the wealth the American colonies no longer brought in before remarking:

> This comparative view of our former territories in America is not stated with any idea of lessening the consequence of a future friendship and connection with them; on the contrary it is to be hoped we shall reap more advantages from their trade as friends than ever we could derive from them as Colonies . . . [16]

And now King George found himself in front of the man whose job it was to help form "friendship and connection" between

Britain and the new nation. He was also a man who had helped tear the British Empire apart.

John Adams made the requisite three "reverences," or bows—the first upon entering the room, the second halfway toward the King, and the third upon stopping in front of His Majesty. The gentleman from Massachusetts then presented his credentials, uttering for the first time: "The United States of America, have appointed me their Minister Plenipotentiary to your Majesty."

Originally intending "to deliver [his] Credentials Silently and retire," Adams had been encouraged by fellow diplomats he met in London to make a speech before the King. He spoke of "restoring an entire esteem, Confidence and Affection, or in better Words, 'the old good Nature and the old good Humour'" between the people of Britain and the new United States.[17]

The King listened politely to Adams before replying that "the Circumstances of this Audience are so extraordinary, the language you have now held is so extremely proper," as to make him favorably disposed to Adams's message of goodwill.

"I will be very frank with you," King George continued. "I was the last to consent to the Seperation. But the Seperation having been made, and having become inevitable, I have always said as I say now, that I would be the first to meet the Friendship of the United States as an independent Power."[18]

After this formal exchange, the King disarmed Adams by remarking in a casual, even laughing manner, that he had heard Adams, who had just come from France, was "not the most attached of all Your Countrymen, to the manners of France."

Adams, truthfully but diplomatically, responded that "that Opinion sir, is not mistaken, I must avow to your Majesty, I have no Attachments but to my own Country."

To this the King responded—"quick as lightning," as Adams remembered—"An honest Man will never have any other."

CONCLUSION

SINCE THE DAYS WHEN EARLY HUMANS FIRST ORGANIZED themselves into groups for mutual protection and assistance, human societies have imposed rules intended to keep order. As societies evolved, those rules were written down and became systems of laws. A society's values are reflected in the system of laws it adopts to protect the rights of its people, and especially how much value that society places on each individual human soul. Sometimes these values are defined in the affirmative—when a society shows what it believes. Our American society does this in the Declaration of Independence. The Continental Congress, which approved this document, was issuing the manifesto of a new society free of British rule, one founded on a revolutionary combination of ideas.

The document leads off by explaining the truths the Congress's members held to be self-evident: that people have certain rights; that government's job is to protect these rights and remain answerable to the people in doing so; and that if government fails at this job the people can adjust it as they see fit. These simple statements in the Declaration's preamble contain thousands of years of human wisdom, distilled and interpreted in the mind of an authentic American genius.

Sometimes, however, just as much can be learned about a society by the values they define in the negative—that is, when they explain what they are definitively against. The Declaration does this, too, in the litany of grievances against King George III. This is why that section of the Declaration deserves consideration on its own, despite not being as rhetorically memorable as the passages that open and close the document. This is one of the imbalances that I have tried to correct in this book.

Most—but I fear increasingly few—Americans can recite the part of the Declaration that shows what America stands *for*, but fewer are familiar with the Founders' explanation, in the same document, of what America stands *against*. American society remains committed to the principles of equality and liberty outlined in the Declaration's first lines. But the grievances listed later should remind us of what we fought against, and what we must not allow ourselves to become.

As we near the first-quarter mark of the twenty-first century, the steady growth of the administrative state under presidents of both political parties has made the central government based in Washington an all-too-common intruder into the lives of most Americans. In many ways, these lessons of the eighteenth century have never been more relevant.

We must remember that the Declaration of Independence is not just a manifesto for natural human rights, but it is a manifesto against a strong central government that would infringe upon those rights. It is against "swarms of officers" that "harass" the people. It is against the unchecked growth of executive power. It is against an administrative state.

The tragedy of American legislative bodies (federal and state) in the twentieth and into the twenty-first century is one of slow and steady unilateral disarmament. Bit by bit, state legislatures have become more comfortable giving up more and more of their power to the federal government. Likewise, the Congress in Washington has turned over much of its power to unelected, unaccountable bureaucrats housed within the executive branch. In many areas where Congress once reigned supreme, it has now been reduced to a token "oversight" role at best.

The steady usurpation of legislative authority by the executive branch, and of state authority by federal authority, is a creeping phenomenon that is in some ways nearly as menacing to American liberty as a royal colonial governor who woke up on the wrong side of his feather bed. And the greatest indignity is that this is a problem largely of our own making. Over the last eight decades, the people's elected representatives have made countless choices that have steadily diminished their own power, and with it that of the people they represent. In many respects, they have done so for a simple, understandable, but indefensible reason: Delegating to others the difficult and contentious task of making law has a tendency to make reelection easier.

What is needed is an innovative, perhaps even a radical reimagining of the relationship between Congress and the executive branch, and between state governments and the federal government. This would be a system in which Congress actually exercises the power and authority it is supposed to, rather than delegating that power to a vast web of government agencies. In such a system, any powers not delegated to the federal government to the Constitution would actually be reserved for the state governments or the people, as the Tenth Amendment promises.

Although it might seem radical to us to put more power back in the hands of legislatures, that's only because we've had blinders on for too long. The Founders' original vision, forged in part by watching their elected legislatures in the colonies get trampled on and dissolved at will by the King's appointed governors, was one that vested as much power as possible in the place where it was closest to the people—the chamber of their elected representatives. And in a republic like ours, isn't that where most of the power should belong?

No other conclusion can be drawn from the colonists' response to the heavy-handed actions of King George III's government. The seeds of revolution were planted when that government, whose ruler combined a devoted British patriotism with a German absolutist idea of monarchy, decided to squeeze its American colonies tighter and tighter.

Those seeds took root when His Majesty's royal governors shut down the colonial legislatures where the people had their only say in government. They grew whenever a citizen was dragged before one of His Majesty's courts without benefit of a jury of his peers—a right any British subject should have enjoyed—or when the courts were shut down altogether due to conflicts with the King's law. They flourished despite the pressure of unfair trade restrictions, attempts to control the free market for products like tea. And finally they bore the fruit of revolution.

Of course, it took the work of several skilled hands to bring that fruit to bear. Thomas Paine's rhetoric lit the fire that would fuel the engines of independence. Edmund Randolph defied his loyalist father and fought with George Washington, then joined his fellow Virginians to lead the charge for breaking all ties with Britain. John Adams used his legal skill to remind the royal courts what justice really meant, and later added his expertise to the drafting of the Declaration. Benjamin Franklin, despite being stricken with gout, helped with the editing—and used his trademark wit to console the main author as the full Congress argued over the draft. It was Thomas Jefferson, of course, whom Franklin consoled—the man who staved off his headaches long enough to focus on the important task at hand, and shake loose from the shelves of his meticulously organized mental library the ancient and modern ideas he would use to explain the Americans' unprecedented act to an astounded world.

These men were not perfect, and neither was the system they created. They were keenly aware that as they signed their names to a statement that "all men are created equal," this was far from the reality for many of their fellow men and women. And for many Americans, it took far too long for this reality to come to pass. Millions of African Americans lived, worked, and died never knowing freedom simply because of the color of their skin, and their descendants in large swaths of the country were forced into second-class citizenry until the latter half of the twentieth century. Millions of Americans were not able to exercise that most precious of the rights of citizenship—the vote—until that same century due to their race or gender. There were the Mormons who were forced out of their communities by government forces because of their religion, and the Japanese Americans who spent years behind barbed wire on American soil because they happened to look like the enemy (even as their sons fought under the Stars and Stripes).

For many in marginalized communities in America to this day, the fight for real equality goes on. But what makes that fight so righteous is that we still look to the words of the Declaration for inspiration. When Jefferson and his colleagues signed their names to that document, they were making a bet on an idea. It's a bet that every succeeding generation of Americans has done its best to make good on.

Sometimes making good on it means expending blood and treasure. In the midst of the greatest struggle we have yet faced to preserve our founding ideals, one of America's greatest leaders turned to the Declaration of Independence for strength. Abraham Lincoln, despite his deep knowledge of and respect for the law rooted in the Constitution, viewed the Declaration as a perfect expression of our founding principles. He felt there was no firmer bedrock on which our nation could stand than the simple truth that "all men are created equal." Indeed, Lincoln observed that he "never had a feeling politically that did not spring from the sentiments embodied in the Declaration of Independence."[1]

In 1854, during his famous series of debates with Stephen Douglas, Lincoln called that concept "the leading principle, the sheet anchor of American republicanism." And he used it to attack the institution of slavery, arguing that if slaves were indeed human, they too had the right to govern themselves according to the Declaration. "If the negro is a man," said Lincoln, "why then my ancient faith teaches me that 'all men are created equal'; and that there can be no moral right in connection with one man's making a slave of another." That, according to Lincoln, was "despotism"— the very charge Jefferson leveled at King George.[2]

Four years later, he told an audience in Chicago that what binds us all together as Americans, whether our families had been here since the founding or came in the latest wave of immigration, was that we could all rally behind the "father of all moral principle"—that doctrine of equality expressed in the Declaration. "That is the electric cord in that Declaration," he said, "that links the hearts of patriotic and liberty-loving men together, that will link those patriotic hearts as long as the love of freedom exists in the minds of men throughout the world."[3] It is recorded that applause erupted after this line—and it is easy to see why.

In February 1861, as he prepared to take over the presidency of a country inching toward war over the question of slavery, Lincoln spent George Washington's birthday in Philadelphia. In a short impromptu speech on the steps of Independence Hall, Lincoln considered the question of what had kept the country united in the decades since its founding. He concluded that the great unifying force was "that sentiment in the Declaration of Independence which gave liberty, not alone to the people of this country, but, I hope, to the world, for all future time."[4]

And in November 1863, as the war to make all Americans free raged around him, Lincoln addressed those gathered to dedicate a cemetery at the site of the recent Battle of Gettysburg. "Four score and seven years ago," he told those assembled, "our fathers brought forth, on this continent, a new nation, conceived in liberty, and dedicated to the proposition that all men are created equal." There was his "ancient faith" again. But now he cast the current struggle in no uncertain terms as an effort to reclaim our founding principles. "Now we are engaged in a great civil war," he said, "testing whether that nation, or any nation so conceived, and so dedicated, can long endure." It was a test that, by God's grace, we passed.

Just as our nation has not always expressed perfectly that ideal of liberty among our fellow men, Lincoln's additional hope that this liberty be expanded across the entire world has sadly remained unfulfilled. But Lincoln understood then what we must understand now—that the Declaration of Independence must be a guiding light, always moving ahead of us, urging us onward, urging us to ever more perfectly follow the principles it sets out.

A century after Lincoln spoke those immortal words at Gettysburg, someone else stood in front of a colossal marble statue of Lincoln and made a proclamation that was no less immortal. "Even though we face the difficulties of today and tomorrow," Dr. Martin Luther King Jr. assured the throngs stretched out before him, "I still have a dream. It is a dream deeply rooted in the American dream." And then he told us what the American dream meant to him. "I have a dream," he said, "that one day this nation will rise up and live out the true meaning of its creed: 'We hold these truths to be self-evident, that all men are created equal.'" The crowd cheered. Dr. King recognized our nation's creed in Jefferson's words, and he was urging us to better live up to it.

This is our task as Americans today, and it will be the task for every future generation. Armed with a greater understanding of the Declaration's principles and how it came to be, we will surely be able to fulfill it.

ACKNOWLEDGMENTS

Once again, it has been an enjoyable process to work with my outstanding editor, Bria Sandford, along with Helen Healey and everyone else at Sentinel. My longtime agents, Keith Urbahn and Matt Latimer, provided inspiration and encouragement—not to mention the considerable talents of their entire team at Javelin, especially Dylan Colligan and Vanessa Santos. I am grateful, as always, to my family for putting up with yet another time-consuming project. Finally, to everyone who has taken a few minutes here and there out of their busy day to read this book, I truly appreciate your time.

NOTES

PREFACE

1. "From George Washington to the Hebrew Congregation in Newport, Rhode Island, 18 August 1790," *Founders Online*, National Archives, last modified June 13, 2018, https://founders.archives.gov/documents/Washington/05-06-02-0135. Original source: *The Papers of George Washington*, Presidential Series, vol. 6, *1 July 1790–30 November 1790*, ed. Mark A. Mastromarino (Charlottesville: University of Virginia Press), 1996, 284–86.

INTRODUCTION

1. Valerie Strauss, "What Americans Don't Know about Their History," *The Washington Post*, July 3, 2010.
2. Strauss, "What Americans Don't Know about Their History."
3. Amy B. Wang, "Some Trump Supporters Thought NPR Tweeted Propaganda. It Was the Declaration of Independence," *The Washington Post*, July 5, 2017, https://www.washingtonpost.com/news/the-fix/wp/2017/07/05/some-trump-supporters-thought-npr-tweeted-propaganda-it-was-the-declaration-of-independence.
4. Frank Newport, "Most in U.S. Still Proud to Be an American," Gallup, July 4, 2013, http://news.gallup.com/poll/163361/proud-american.aspx.

CHAPTER ONE

1. "From Thomas Jefferson to James Madison, 30 August 1823," *Founders Online*, National Archives, last modified June 13, 2018, https://founders.archives.gov/documents/Jefferson/98-01-02-3728.

2. "From Thomas Jefferson to Nathaniel Macon, December 4, 1818," Online Library of Liberty, citing Jefferson, *The Works of Thomas Jefferson*, Federal Edition, vol. 12, footnote 1 (New York and London: G.P. Putnam's Sons, 1904–5), http://oll.libertyfund.org/titles/808.

3. "From Thomas Jefferson to Nathaniel Macon, December 4, 1818."

4. Thomas Jefferson, "An Anecdote of Dr. Franklin," History.org, Colonial Williamsburg, http://www.history.org/almanack/resources/jeffersonanecdote.cfm.

5. "Hessians," MountVernon.org, Washington Library, MountVernon.org, Washington Library, Center for Digital History, https://www.mountvernon.org/library/digitalhistory/digital-encyclopedia/article/hessians.

6. "From John Adams to Timothy Pickering, 6 August 1822," *Founders Online*, National Archives, last modified June 13, 2018, https://founders.archives.gov/documents/Adams/99-02-02-7674.

7. Julian Boyd, *The Declaration of Independence: The Evolution of the Text* (Washington, D.C.: Library of Congress/Thomas Jefferson Memorial Foundation, Inc., 1999), 35.

8. *Journals of the Continental Congress, 1774–1789*, vol. 5, eds. Worthington Chauncey Ford, Gaillard Hunt, John Clement Fitzpatrick, Roscoe R. Hill, Kenneth E. Harris, Steven D. Tilley (Washington, D.C.: Government Printing Office, 1906), 516.

9. Jon Meacham, *Thomas Jefferson: The Art of Power* (New York: Random House, 2012), 106.

10. *The Pennsylvania Magazine of History and Biography*, vol. 1 (Philadelphia: Historical Society of Pennsylvania, 1877).

11. "July Highlight: George Rejected and Liberty Protected," Harvard University Declaration Resources Project, *Course of Human Events, Declaration Resources Project Blog*, July 4, 2016, https://declaration.fas.harvard.edu/blog/july-proclamations.

12. "To John Adams from Benjamin Rush, 20 July 1811," *Founders Online*, National Archives, last modified June 13, 2018, https://founders.archives.gov/documents/Adams/99-02-02-5659.

13. "To John Adams from Benjamin Rush, 20 July 1811."

CHAPTER TWO

1. "Great Britain: Parliament—The Declaratory Act; March 18, 1766," Yale Law School, The Avalon Project, http://avalon.law.yale.edu/18th_century/declaratory_act_1766.asp.

2. "Massachusetts Circular Letter to the Colonial Legislatures; February 11, 1768," Yale Law School, The Avalon Project, http://avalon.law.yale.edu/18th_century/mass_circ_let_1768.asp.

3. "Massachusetts Circular Letter to the Colonial Legislatures; February 11, 1768."

4. Dumas Malone, *Jefferson and His Time, vol. 1: Jefferson the Virginian* (Charlottesville, VA: University of Virginia Press, 1948), 136.
5. Quoted in George Bancroft, *History of the United States, from the Discovery of the American Continent*, vol. 3 (New York: Appleton, 1896), 248.
6. Quoted in George Bancroft, *History of the United States*, 239.
7. Mark Puls, *Samuel Adams: Father of the American Revolution* (New York: St. Martin's Press, 2006), 68.
8. *Journals of the House of Representatives of Massachusetts, 1715–1779*, vol. 44 (Boston: Massachusetts Historical Society, 1919–1990), 148.
9. "The House of Representatives' Circular Letter to the Speakers of the Colonial Assemblies," February 11, 1768, Colonial Society of Massachusetts, https://www.colonialsociety.org/node/2932.
10. "Massachusetts Circular Letter to the Colonial Legislatures; February 11, 1768."
11. "Massachusetts Circular Letter to the Colonial Legislatures; February 11, 1768."
12. "Massachusetts Circular Letter to the Colonial Legislatures; February 11, 1768."
13. "Massachusetts Circular Letter to the Colonial Legislatures; February 11, 1768."
14. Puls, *Samuel Adams: Father of the American Revolution*, 74.
15. Quoted in George Bancroft, *History of the United States*, 284.
16. Quoted in George Bancroft, *History of the United States*, 285.
17. *Journals of the House of Representatives of Massachusetts*, 1715–1779, vol. 45, 88.
18. "History of the Old State House," BostonHistory.org, http://www.bostonhistory.org/history.
19. *Journals of the House of Representatives of Massachusetts*, 1715–1779, vol. 45, 89.
20. *Journals of the House of Representatives of Massachusetts*, 1715–1779, vol. 45, 89.
21. *Journals of the House of Representatives of Massachusetts*, 1715–1779, vol. 45, 94.
22. Puls, *Samuel Adams: Father of the American Revolution*, 83.
23. Quoted in Puls, *Samuel Adams: Father of the American Revolution*, 83.
24. *Journals of the House of Representatives of Massachusetts*, 1715–1779, vol. 45, 92.
25. "Jefferson's Height," Monticello.org, an article courtesy of the Thomas Jefferson Encyclopedia, https://www.monticello.org/site/research-and-collections/jeffersons-height.
26. Jon Meacham, *Thomas Jefferson: The Art of Power* (New York: Random House, 2012), 44.
27. *Virginia Gazette*, December 15, 1768, 2, History.org, Colonial Williamsburg, http://research.history.org/DigitalLibrary/va-gazettes/VGSinglePage.cfm?issueIDNo=68.R.46&page=2&res=LO.
28. *Virginia Gazette*, December 15, 1768, 2.
29. *Journals of the House of Burgesses of Virginia, 1766–1769*, ed. John Pendleton Kennedy (Richmond, Va.: The Colonial Press, E. Waddey Co., 1906), 189.
30. "Norborne Berkeley, Baron de Botetourt (1717–1770)," Encyclopedia Virginia, https://www.encyclopediavirginia.org/Berkeley_Norborne_baron_de_Botetourt_1717-1770#start_entry.

31. *Journals of the House of Burgesses of Virginia, 1766–1769,* 189–90.
32. *Journals of the House of Burgesses of Virginia, 1766–1769,* 214.
33. *Journals of the House of Burgesses of Virginia, 1766–1769,* 214.
34. *Journals of the House of Burgesses of Virginia, 1766–1769,* 214.
35. *Journals of the House of Burgesses of Virginia, 1766–1769,* 214.
36. "Jefferson's Autobiography," Yale Law School, The Avalon Project, http://avalon .law.yale.edu/19th_century/jeffauto.asp.
37. *Jefferson the Virginian,* vol. XXXX, 136.
38. *Jefferson the Virginian,* vol. XXXX, 136.
39. "Jefferson's Autobiography."
40. "[May 1769]," *Founders Online,* National Archives, last modified June 13, 2018, https://founders.archives.gov/documents/Washington/01-02-02-0004-0013. Original source: *The Diaries of George Washington,* vol. 2, *14 January 1766–31 December 1770,* ed. Donald Jackson (Charlottesville: University Press of Virginia, 1976), 146–54.
41. "Virginia Nonimportation Resolutions, 17 May 1769," *Founders Online,* National Archives, last modified June 13, 2018, https://founders.archives.gov /documents/Jefferson/01-01-02-0019. Original source: The Papers of Thomas Jefferson, vol. 1, 1760–1776, ed. Julian P. Boyd (Princeton: Princeton University Press, 1950), 27–31.

CHAPTER THREE

1. *Legal Papers of John Adams,* vol. 2, note 9, Massachusetts Historical Society, http://www.masshist.org/publications/adams-papers/index.php/view /ADMS-05-02-02-0006-0004-0001#LJA02d042n9.
2. Noel Rae, *The People's War: Original Voices of the American Revolution* (Guilford, Conn.: Globe Pequot Press, 2012), 72.
3. Neal Nusholtz, "How John Adams Won the Hancock Trial," *Journal of the American Revolution,* August 30, 2016, AllThingsLiberty.com, http://allthingsliberty .com/2016/08/john-adams-won-hancock-trial.
4. *A Companion to John Adams and John Quincy Adams,* David Waldstreicher, ed. (Malden, Mass., and Oxford, UK: Wiley-Blackwell, 2013), 72.
5. Anne Husted Burleigh, *John Adams* (New York: Routledge, 2017), 85.
6. "The Vice Admiralty Courts," The Declaration of Independence, USHistory .org, http://www.ushistory.org/declaration/related/vac.html.
7. *Legal Papers of John Adams,* vol. 2.
8. "Madeira," MountVernon.org, Washington Library, Center for Digital History, https://www.mountvernon.org/library/digitalhistory/digital-encyclopedia /article/madeira.
9. *A Companion to John Adams and John Quincy Adams,* 72.

10. "Adams' Copy of the Information and Draft of His Argument: Court of Vice Admiralty, Boston, October 1768–March 1769," *Founders Online,* National Archives, last modified June 13, 2018, https://founders.archives.gov/documents/Adams/05-02-02-0006-0004-0002. Original source: *The Adams Papers,* Legal Papers of John Adams, vol. 2, Cases 31–62, eds. L. Kinvin Wroth and Hiller B. Zobel (Cambridge, Mass. Harvard University Press, 1965), 194–210.

11. West Virginia Association for Justice, "Trial by Jury: 'Inherent and invaluable,'" http://www.wvaj.org/index.cfm?pg=HistoryTrialbyJury.

12. *Legal Papers of John Adams,* vol. 2.

13. Burleigh, *John Adams,* 87.

14. "Adams' Copy of the Information and Draft of His Argument: Court of Vice Admiralty, Boston, October 1768–March 1769."

15. "Adams' Copy of the Information and Draft of His Argument: Court of Vice Admiralty, Boston, October 1768–March 1769."

16. "Adams' Copy of the Information and Draft of His Argument: Court of Vice Admiralty, Boston, October 1768–March 1769."

17. "The Federalist Papers: No. 48," Yale Law School, The Avalon Project, http://avalon.law.yale.edu/18th_century/fed48.asp.

CHAPTER FOUR

1. "Minutes of the Lower House of the North Carolina General Assembly," October 23, 1769–November 6, 1769, vol. 8, 105–41, Documenting the American South, Colonial and State Records of North Carolina, http://docsouth.unc.edu/csr/index.php/document/csr08-0068.

2. "Resolves of the House of Burgesses, Passed the 16th of May, 1769," Encyclopedia Virginia, https://www.encyclopediavirginia.org/media_player?mets_filename=evr3808mets.xml.

3. William S. Powell, "Regulator Movement," NCPedia, 2006, https://www.ncpedia.org/history/colonial/regulator-movement.

4. Edward, Dumbauld, *The Declaration of Independence and What It Means Today* (Norman, Oklahoma: University of Oklahoma Press, 1950), 108.

5. Dumbauld, *The Declaration of Independence and What It Means Today,* 108.

6. Dumbauld, *The Declaration of Independence and What It Means Today,* 109.

7. Dumbauld, *The Declaration of Independence and What It Means Today,* 109.

8. Dumbauld, *The Declaration of Independence and What It Means Today,* 109.

9. Dumbauld, *The Declaration of Independence and What It Means Today,* 109.

10. Donald R., Lennon, "Attachment Clause," NCPedia, 2006, https://www.ncpedia.org/attachment-clause.

11. Lennon, "Attachment Clause."

12. Herbert Friedenwald, *The Declaration of Independence* (New York: Macmillan, 1904), 231.
13. Dumbauld, *The Declaration of Independence and What It Means Today*, 111.
14. Dumbauld, *The Declaration of Independence and What It Means Today*, 111–12.
15. Vernon O. Stumpf, "Martin, Josiah," NCPedia, 1991, https://www.ncpedia .org/biography/martin-josiah.
16. Stumpf, "Martin, Josiah."
17. Stumpf, "Martin, Josiah."
18. Jonathan Martin, "Royal Governor Josiah Martin (1737–1786)," North Carolina History Project, NorthCarolinaHistory.org, http://northcarolinahistory .org/encyclopedia/royal-governor-josiah-martin-1737-1786.
19. Vernon O. Stumpf, "Josiah Martin and His Search for Success: The Road to North Carolina," North Carolina Office of Archives and History, Colonial Records Project, vol. 53 (1976), 55–79, http://www.ncpublications.com/colonial /nchr/Subjects/stumpf.htm.
20. Stumpf, "Martin, Josiah."
21. Daniel W. Barefoot, "Tryon Palace," NCPedia, 2006, https://www.ncpedia.org /tryon-palace.
22. "Tryon Palace," North Carolina History Project, NorthCarolinaHistory.org, http://northcarolinahistory.org/encyclopedia/tryon-palace.
23. Barefoot, "Tryon Palace."
24. Quoted in "Tryon Palace," North Carolina History Project.
25. Quoted in Barefoot, "Tryon Palace."
26. Barefoot, "Tryon Palace."
27. "Letter from Josiah Martin to William Legge, Earl of Dartmouth," February 26, 1773, Documenting the American South, Colonial and State Records of North Carolina, http://docsouth.unc.edu/csr/index.php/document/csr09 -0166.
28. "Letter from Josiah Martin to William Legge, Earl of Dartmouth," February 26, 1773.
29. "Letter from Josiah Martin to William Legge, Earl of Dartmouth," February 26, 1773.
30. "Minutes of the Upper House of the North Carolina General Assembly," January 25, 1773–March 6, 1773, vol. 9, 376–447, Documenting the American South, Colonial and State Records of North Carolina, http://docsouth.unc.edu /csr/index.php/document/csr09-0169.
31. "Minutes of the Upper House of the North Carolina General Assembly," January 25, 1773–March 6, 1773.
32. "Minutes of the Upper House of the North Carolina General Assembly," January 25, 1773–March 6, 1773.
33. "Minutes of the Upper House of the North Carolina General Assembly," January 25, 1773–March 6, 1773.

34. "Letter from Josiah Martin to William Legge, Earl of Dartmouth," February 26, 1773.
35. "Letter from Josiah Martin to William Legge, Earl of Dartmouth," February 26, 1773.
36. "Letter from Josiah Martin to William Legge, Earl of Dartmouth," February 26, 1773.
37. Friedenwald, *The Declaration of Independence*, 232.
38. Milton Ready, *The Tar Heel State: A History of North Carolina* (Columbia: University of South Carolina Press, 2005), 105.
39. Ready, *The Tar Heel State*, 105.
40. "Letter from Josiah Martin to William Legge, Earl of Dartmouth," March 12, 1773, Documenting the American South, Colonial and State Records of North Carolina, http://docsouth.unc.edu/csr/index.php/document/csr09-0177.
41. "Letter from Josiah Martin to William Legge, Earl of Dartmouth," March 12, 1773.
42. "Letter from Josiah Martin to William Legge, Earl of Dartmouth," March 12, 1773.
43. Friedenwald, *The Declaration of Independence*, 232.
44. Ready, *The Tar Heel State*, 105.
45. "Journal of Josiah Quincy," March 26, 1773–April 5, 1773, vol. 9, 610–13, Documenting the American South, Colonial and State Records of North Carolina, http://docsouth.unc.edu/csr/index.php/document/csr09-0180.
46. Friedenwald, *The Declaration of Independence*, 230.
47. Sydney George Fisher, "The Twenty-Eight Charges Against the King in the Declaration of Independence," *The Pennsylvania Magazine of History and Biography* 31, no. 3 (1907), 257–303, https://www.jstor.org/stable/pdf/20085387.pdf?refreqid=excelsior:345c4cebe95fc2281cb9447d71222b4c.
48. "1776: Hutchinson, Strictures upon the Declaration of Independence," Online Library of Liberty, http://oll.libertyfund.org/pages/1776-hutchinson-strictures-upon-the-declaration-of-independence.
49. "Jefferson's 'Original Rough Draught' of the Declaration of Independence," Declaring Independence: Drafting the Documents, Library of Congress, http://www.loc.gov/exhibits/declara/ruffdrft.html. Original source: *The Papers of Thomas Jefferson*, vol. 1, *1760–1776*, ed. Julian P. Boyd (Princeton NJ: Princeton University Press, 1950), 243–47.
50. Julian Boyd, *The Declaration of Independence: The Evolution of the Text* (Washington, D.C.: Library of Congress/Thomas Jefferson Memorial Foundation, Inc., 1999), 33, n. 54.
51. *Worcester v. Georgia*, Oyez, https://www.oyez.org/cases/1789-1850/31us515.
52. *Worcester v. Georgia*.
53. Tim Alan Garrison, *Worcester v. Georgia* (1832), New Georgia Encyclopedia, Government and Politics, U.S. Supreme Court Cases, April 27, 2004, http://

www.georgiaencyclopedia.org/articles/government-politics/worcester-v
-georgia-1832.
54. "Executive Orders, Harry S. Truman, 1945–1953," Harry S. Truman Presidential Library & Museum, https://www.trumanlibrary.org/executiveorders
/index.php?pid=180.
55. Joshua Waimberg, "Youngstown Steel: The Supreme Court Stands Up to the
President," *Constitution Daily Blog,* National Constitution Center, November
16, 2015, https://constitutioncenter.org/blog/youngstown-steel-the-supreme
-court-stands-up-to-the-president.
56. *Youngstown Sheet & Tube Co. v. Sawyer,* 343 U.S. 579 (1952), Justica, U.S.
Supreme Court, https://supreme.justia.com/cases/federal/us/343/579/case.html.
57. Waimberg, "Youngstown Steel: The Supreme Court Stands Up to the President."

CHAPTER FIVE

1. "Philadelphia, September 29. Extract of a letter from London, August 4," Massachusetts Historical Society, https://www.masshist.org/revolution/image-viewer
.php?item_id=401&img_step=1&tpc=&pid=2&mode=transcript&tpc=&pid
=2#page1. Original source: *The Massachusetts Gazette,* 3; and *The Boston Post-Boy
and Advertiser,* no. 842, October 4–11, 1773.
2. "The following was dispersed in Hand Bills among the worthy Citizens of Philadelphia," Massachusetts Historical Society, https://www.masshist.org/revolution
/image-viewer.php?item_id=417&img_step=1&tpc=&mode=transcript&tpc
=#page1. Original source, *The Boston-Gazette,* number 968, October 25, 1773, 2.
3. "Philadelphia, September 29. Extract of a letter from London, August 4."
4. "The Boston Tea Party: Introduction," Massachusetts Historical Society,
https://www.masshist.org/revolution/teaparty.php.
5. "Disguise of Sons of Liberty," Boston Tea Party Ships and Museum, www
.bostonteapartyship.com/boston=tea=party=disguise.
6. "Announcement of the Boston Tea Party, December 20, 1773," Presentations and
Activities, Library of Congress, http://www.loc.gov/teachers/classroommaterials
/presentationsandactivities/presentations/timeline/amrev/rebelln/tea.html.
Original source, *The Boston Gazette,* December 20, 1773.
7. Peter D. G. Thomas, *Tea Party to Independence: The Third Phase of the American
Revolution, 1773–1776* (London: Clarendon Press, 1991), 20.
8. The editors of the Encyclopaedia Britannica, "Boston Tea Party," Britannica
Academic, www.britannica.com/event/Boston-Tea-Party.
9. Thomas Whately, *Regulations Lately Made Concerning the Colonies* (London:
J. Wilkie, 1765).
10. Stephen Hopkins, *The Rights of Colonies Examined,* Evans Early American Imprint
Collection, http://quod.lib.umich.edu/cgi/t/text/text-idx?c=evans;cc=evans;vie
w=text;idno=N07846.0001.001;rgn=div1;node=N07846.0001.001%3A2, 4.

11. Hopkins, *The Rights of Colonies Examined*, 22.
12. Thomas Williams Bicknell, *The History of the State of Rhode Island and Providence Plantations*, vol. 3 (New York: The American Historical Society, 1920), 1083.
13. "The following was dispersed in Hand Bills among the worthy Citizens of Philadelphia."
14. "The following was dispersed in Hand Bills among the worthy Citizens of Philadelphia."
15. Alvin Rabushka, *Taxation in Colonial America* (Princeton: Princeton University Press, 2008), 867.
16. "The Secret Plan," December 16, 1773, Boston Tea Party Ships and Museum, http://www.bostonteapartyship.com/the-secret-plan.
17. Thomas Paine, *Rights of Man*, http://www.gutenberg.org/files/3742/3742-h /3742-h.htm.
18. Jason Russell, "Look at How Many Pages Are in the Federal Tax Code," *Washington Examiner*, April 15, 2016.

CHAPTER SIX

1. Eugene S. Ferguson, *Truxtun of the Constellation: The Life of Commodore Thomas Truxtun, U.S. Navy, 1755–1822* (Baltimore: John Hopkins University Press, 1956), 19.
2. Ferguson, *Truxtun of the Constellation*, 18–19.
3. Ferguson, *Truxtun of the Constellation*, 19.
4. Ferguson, *Truxtun of the Constellation*, 20.
5. "A Collection of All the Statutes Now in Force" (London: C. Eyre and W. Strahan, 1780).
6. "Major Mark Park," New York City Department of Parks and Recreation, https://www.nycgovparks.org/parks/major-mark-park/history.
7. *Naval Biography: Consisting of Memoirs of the Most Distinguished Officers of the American Navy* (Cincinnati: Morgan, Williams & Co., 1815), 27.
8. *Naval Biography*, 27.
9. Ferguson, *Truxtun of the Constellation*, 18.
10. Nicholas Tracy, *Manila Ransomed: The British Assault on Manila in the Seven Years War* (Liverpool: Liverpool University Press, 1995), 76.
11. Ferguson, *Truxtun of the Constellation*, 20.
12. Ferguson, *Truxtun of the Constellation*, 21.
13. *Pennsylvania Gazette*, February 21, 1776, 3.
14. "[Notes of Debates in the Continental Congress] Oct. 3 [i.e. 4]," note 1, *Founders Online*, National Archives, last modified June 13, 2018, founders .archives.gov/documents/Adams/01-02-02-0005-0004-0001. Original source: *The Adams Papers, Diary and Autobiography of John Adams*, vol. 2, *1771–1781*, ed. L. H. Butterfield (Cambridge, Mass.: Harvard University Press, 1961), 188–92.

15. "IV. The Declaration as Adopted by Congress [6 July 1775]," *Founders Online,* National Archives, last modified June 13, 2018, https://founders.archives.gov/ documents/Jefferson/01-01-02-0113-0005. Original source: *The Papers of Thomas Jefferson,* vol. 1, *1760–1776,* ed. Julian P. Boyd (Princeton: Princeton University Press, 1950), 213–19.

16. "[Notes of Debates in the Continental Congress] Oct. 3 [i.e. 4]," note 1.

17. "[Notes of Debates in the Continental Congress] Oct. 3 [i.e. 4]," note 1.

18. "[Notes of Debates in the Continental Congress] Oct. 3 [i.e. 4]," note 1.

19. "[October 1775]," *Founders Online,* National Archives, last modified June 13, 2018, https://founders.archives.gov/documents/Adams/01-02-02-0005-0004. Original source: *The Adams Papers,* Diary and Autobiography of John Adams, vol. 2, 188–220.

20. Jim Schmidt, "John J. Zubly (1724–1781)," New Georgia Encyclopedia, History and Archaeology, Colonial Era, 1733–1775, September 12, 2002, http://www.georgiaencyclopedia.org/articles/history-archaeology/john-j -zubly-1724-1781.

21. "To Benjamin Franklin from [David Hartley], 23 November 1775," *Founders Online,* National Archives, last modified June 13, 2018, https://founders. archives.gov/documents/Franklin/01-22-02-0159. Original source: *The Papers of Benjamin Franklin,* vol. 22, *March 23, 1775, through October 27, 1776,* ed. William B. Willcox (New Haven, Conn.: Yale University Press, 1982), 267–68.

22. "James Wilson (1742–1748)," Dickinson College Archives and Special Collections, 2018. archives.dickinson.edu/people/james-wilson-1742-1798.

23. "[Notes of Debates in the Continental Congress] [February 1776]," note 1, *Founders Online,* National Archives, last modified June 13, 2018, https://founders .archives.gov/documents/Adams/01-02-02-0006-0002. Original source: The Adams Papers, Diary and Autobiography of John Adams, vol. 2, 229–34.

24. "[Notes of Debates in the Continental Congress] [February 1776]," note 1.

25. "From John Adams to Horatio Gates," 23 March, 1776, *Founders Online,* National Archives, last modified June 13, 2018, https://founders.archives.gov/documents /Adams/06-04-02-0023. Original source: *The Adams Papers,* Papers of John Adams, vol. 4, *February–August 1776,* ed. Robert J. Taylor (Cambridge, MA: Harvard University Press, 1979), 58–60.

26. "From John Adams to Horatio Gates," 23 March, 1776.

27. "Sender: Richard Henry Lee; Recipient: Landon Carter, Philadelphia, 1st April 1776," Lee Family Digital Archive, https://leefamilyarchive.org/papers /letters/transcripts-gw%20delegates/DIV0275.html.

28. *Journals of the Continental Congress, 1774–1789,* vol. 4, eds. Worthington Chauncey Ford, Gaillard Hunt, John Clement Fitzpatrick, Roscoe R. Hill, Kenneth E. Harris, Steven D. Tilley (Washington, D.C.: Government Printing Office, 1906), 257–58.

29. "The Slave Trade and the Revolution," The Schomburg Center for Research in Black Culture, New York Public Library, http://abolition.nypl.org/essays /us_constitution/2.

30. Edmund C. Burnett, *Letters of Members of the Continental Congress, August 29, 1774 to July 4, 1776,* vol. 1 (Washington, D.C.: Carnegie Institution, 1921), 415.

31. Burnett, *Letters of Members of the Continental Congress, August 29, 1774, to July 4, 1776,* 417.

CHAPTER SEVEN

1. Jill Lepore, "The Sharpened Quill," *The New Yorker,* October 16, 2016.

2. Richard M. Ketchum, *The Winter Soldiers: The Battles for Trenton and Princeton* (New York: Owl Books, 1999), 4.

3. Craig Nelson, *Thomas Paine: Enlightenment, Revolution, and the Birth of Modern Nations* (New York: Viking Penguin, 2006), 53.

4. Nelson, *Thomas Paine,* 77.

5. Nelson, *Thomas Paine,* 77.

6. Nelson, *Thomas Paine,* 76.

7. Thomas Paine, *The Crisis,* November 21, 1778, http://www.gutenberg.org/files /3741/3741-h/3741-h.htm.

8. Nelson, *Thomas Paine,* 89.

9. Quoted in Nelson, *Thomas Paine,* 69.

10. Pauline Maier, *American Scripture: Making the Declaration of Independence* (New York: Knopf, 1997), 31.

11. Lepore, "The Sharpened Quill."

12. "To Thomas Jefferson from Thomas Nelson, Jr., 4 February 1776," *Founders Online,* National Archives, last modified June 13, 2018, https://founders .archives.gov/documents/Jefferson/01-01-02-0148. Original source: *The Papers of Thomas Jefferson,* vol. 1, *1760–1776,* ed. Julian P. Boyd (Princeton: Princeton University Press, 1950), 285–86.

13. This is based on a calculation made by Richard Gimbel in 1956. Richard Gimbel, *A Bibliographical Checklist of Common Sense, with an Account of Its Publication* (New Haven, Conn.: Yale University Press, 1956); Thomas Paine, "The Crisis No. VII," *Pennsylvania Packet.*

14. Lepore, "The Sharpened Quill."

15. Quoted in Nelson, *Thomas Paine,* 93.

16. "From Thomas Jefferson to Francis Eppes, 19 January 1821," *Founders Online,* National Archives, last modified June 13, 2018, https://founders.archives.gov /documents/Jefferson/98-01-02-1778.

17. Lepore, "The Sharpened Quill."

18. Lepore, "The Sharpened Quill."
19. Nelson, *Thomas Paine*, 97.

CHAPTER EIGHT

1. Quoted in Hugh Blair Grigsby, *The Virginia Convention of 1776* (Richmond, Va.: J. W. Randolph, 1855), 7.
2. "The General Assembly Adjourns, 1776," Encyclopedia Virginia, http://www.encyclopediavirginia.org/The_General_Assembly_Adjourns_1776.
3. John Burk, *The History of Virginia: From Its First Settlement to the Present Day*, vol. 4 (Petersburg, Va.: M. W. Dunnavant, 1816), 138, http://amarch.lib.niu.edu/islandora/object/niu-amarch%3A101264.
4. Quoted in "Final Meeting of the House of Burgesses ("Finis" Document), May 6, 1776," Education@Library of Virginia, edu.lva.virginia.gov/online_classroom/shaping_the_constitution/doc/finis.
5. Burk, *The History of Virginia*.
6. "The General Assembly Adjourns, 1776."
7. Grigsby, *The Virginia Convention of 1776*, 36.
8. Bruce Baskerville, "So Brave Etruria Grew," in *Crowns and Colonies: European Monarchies and Overseas Empires*, eds. Robert Aldrich and Cindy McCreery (Manchester, UK: Manchester University Press, 2016).
9. "Edmund Randolph to Thomas Jefferson, 8 May 1813," *Founders Online*, National Archives, last modified June 13, 2018, https://founders.archives.gov/documents/Jefferson/03-06-02-0105. Original source: *The Papers of Thomas Jefferson*, Retirement Series, vol. 6, *11 March to 27 November 1813*, ed. J. Jefferson Looney (Princeton: Princeton University Press, 2009), 108–9.
10. John E. Selby, *The Revolution in Virginia, 1775–1783* (Charlottesville: University of Virginia Press, 2007), 95.
11. Quoted in Grigsby, *The Virginia Convention of 1776*, 16.
12. Quoted in Selby, *The Revolution in Virginia*, 94.
13. Quoted in John Hampden Hazelton, *The Declaration of Independence* (New York: Dodd, Mead, 1906), 400.
14. Selby, *The Revolution in Virginia*, 95–96.
15. Quoted in *The National Centennial Commemoration: Proceedings on the One Hundredth Anniversary of the Introduction and Adoption of the "Resolutions Respecting Independency"* (Philadelphia: n.p., 1876), 25.
16. "Preamble and Resolution of the Virginia Convention, May 15, 1776," Yale Law School, The Avalon Project, http://avalon.law.yale.edu/18th_century/const02.asp.
17. Quoted in Edmund Jennings Lee, *Lee of Virginia, 1642–1892* (Philadelphia: Genealogical Publishing, 1895), 169.

18. "Fryday, May 10. 1776," in "John Adams autobiography, part 1," through 1776, sheet 35 of 53, 11 April–16 May 1776, Massachusetts Historical Society, https://www.masshist.org/digitaladams/archive/doc?id=A1_35.

19. "Fryday, May 10. 1776."

20. "From Thomas Jefferson to Thomas Nelson, 16 May 1776," *Founders Online*, National Archives, last modified June 13, 2018, https://founders.archives.gov /documents/Jefferson/01-01-02-0153. Original source: *The Papers of Thomas Jefferson*, vol. 1, *1760–1776*, ed. Julian P. Boyd (Princeton: Princeton University Press, 1950).

21. Selby, *The Revolution in Virginia*, 97.

22. "From Thomas Jefferson to Thomas Nelson, 16 May 1776."

23. Patrick Glennon, "The Philly Home Where the Declaration of Independence Was Born," *The Philadelphia Inquirer*, September 15, 2007, http://www.philly .com/philly/opinion/commentary/the-philly-home-where-jefferson-took -pen-in-hand-20170915.html.

24. Jon Meacham, *Thomas Jefferson: The Art of Power* (New York: Random House, 2012), 103.

25. "Declaration of Independence Desk," Monticello.org, an article courtesy of the Thomas Jefferson Encyclopedia, https://www.monticello.org/site/research-and -collections/declaration-independence-desk.

26. Patrick Glennon, "The Philly Home Where the Declaration of Independence Was Born."

27. "Lee's Resolutions," Yale Law School, The Avalon Project, http://avalon.law .yale.edu/18th_century/lee.asp.

28. "Jefferson's Autobiography," Yale Law School, The Avalon Project, http://avalon .law.yale.edu/19th_century/jeffauto.asp.

29. "From John Adams to Timothy Pickering, 6 August 1822," *Founders Online*, National Archives, last modified June 13, 2018, https://founders.archives.gov /documents/Adams/99-02-02-7674.

30. "From John Adams to Timothy Pickering, 6 August 1822."

31. "From Thomas Jefferson to James Madison, 30 August 1823," *Founders Online*, National Archives, last modified June 13, 2018, https://founders.archives.gov /documents/Jefferson/98-01-02-3728.

32. "From Thomas Jefferson to Benjamin Franklin, [21 June 1776]," *Founders Online*, National Archives, last modified June 13, 2018, https://founders.archives .gov/documents/Jefferson/01-01-02-0168. Original source: *The Papers of Thomas Jefferson*, vol. 1, *1760–1776*, 404–6.

33. "From John Adams to Timothy Pickering, 6 August 1822."

34. "1774 to 1783," Thomas Jefferson Papers, 1606 to 1827, Library of Congress, https://www.loc.gov/collections/thomas-jefferson-papers/articles-and -essays/the-thomas-jefferson-papers-timeline-1743-to-1827/1774-to-1783.

35. "From Thomas Jefferson to James Madison, 30 August 1823."

36. "From John Adams to Timothy Pickering, 6 August 1822."

37. Julian Boyd, *The Declaration of Independence: The Evolution of the Text* (Washington, D.C.: Library of Congress/Thomas Jefferson Memorial Foundation, Inc., 1999), 28.

38. Walter Isaacson, "Declaring Independence: How They Chose These Words," *Time,* July 7, 2003, http://content.time.com/time/magazine/article/0,9171, 1005150-1,00.html.

39. "From Thomas Jefferson to Benjamin Franklin, [21 June 1776]."

40. "To George Washington from Benjamin Franklin, 21 June 1776," *Founders Online,* National Archives, last modified June 13, 2018, https://founders.archives .gov/documents/Washington/03-05-02-0036. Original source: *The Papers of George Washington*, Revolutionary War Series, vol. 5, 16 June 1776–12 August 1776, ed. Philander D. Chase (Charlottesville: University Press of Virginia, 1993), 64–65.

41. "From John Adams to Timothy Pickering, 6 August 1822."

42. "From Thomas Jefferson to James Madison, 30 August 1823."

43. Boyd, *The Declaration of Independence,* 35.

44. Boyd, *The Declaration of Independence,* 32.

45. Boyd, *The Declaration of Independence,* 27.

46. Boyd, *The Declaration of Independence,* 27.

CHAPTER NINE

1. "Jefferson's 'original Rough draught' of the Declaration of Independence," Declaring Independence: Drafting the Documents, Library of Congress, https://www.loc.gov/exhibits/declara/ruffdrft.html. Original source: *The Papers of Thomas Jefferson*, vol. 1, *1760–1776*, ed. Julian P. Boyd (Princeton: Princeton University Press, 1950), 243–47.

2. "Jefferson's Autobiography," Yale Law School, The Avalon Project, http://avalon .law.yale.edu/19th_century/jeffauto.asp.

3. Julian Boyd, *The Declaration of Independence: The Evolution of the Text* (Washington, D.C.: Library of Congress/Thomas Jefferson Memorial Foundation, Inc., 1999), 35.

4. "From John Adams to Timothy Pickering, 6 August 1822," *Founders Online,* National Archives, last modified June 13, 2018, https://founders.archives.gov /documents/Adams/99-02-02-7674.

5. "Jefferson's Autobiography."

6. William M. S. Rasmussen, "Thomas Jefferson's Declaration of Independence— The First Draft & Its Paragraph about Slavery," Virginia Repertory Theater. *Behind the Scenes Blog,* October 3, 2016, http://www.va-rep.org/blog/2016/10 /03/thomas-jeffersons-declaration-of-independence-the-first-draft-its -paragraph-about-slavery.

7. "The Ordinance of 1784," History, Art, and Archives, United States House of Representatives, http://history.house.gov/Historical-Highlights/1700s/Ordinance-of-1784.
8. "From Thomas Jefferson to John Holmes, 22 April 1820," *Founders Online*, National Archives, last modified June 13, 2018, https://founders.archives.gov/documents/Jefferson/98-01-02-1234.
9. Frederick Douglass, "What to the Slave Is the 4th of July," speech delivered on July 4, 1852, Rochester, New York, American Rhetoric Online Speech Bank, http://www.americanrhetoric.com/speeches/frederickdouglassslaveto4thofjuly.htm.
10. Douglass, "What to the Slave Is the 4th of July."

CHAPTER TEN

1. Jared Keller, "How the Declaration of Independence Went Viral," *Pacific Standard*, June 28, 2016, https://psmag.com/news/how-the-declaration-of-independence-went-viral.
2. "Edmund Burke, Speech on Conciliation with the Colonies," March 22, 1775, The Founders' Constitution, chapter 1, http://press-pubs.uchicago.edu/founders/documents/v1ch1s2.html.
3. Edmund Burke, remarks in Parliament, December 14, 1778, quoted in Alexander Charles Ewald, *Leaders in the Senate: A Biographical History of the Rise and Development of the British Constitution* (London: William Mackenzie, 1884), 195.
4. Richard Cavendish, "The Coronation of George III," *History Today* 61, no. 9 (September 2011), https://www.historytoday.com/richard-cavendish/coronation-george-iii.
5. "September Highlight: Extravagant and Inadmissible Claim of Independency," King George III, speech to Parliament, October 31, 1776, Harvard University Declaration Resources Project, *Course of Human Events, Declaration Resources Project Blog*, https://declaration.fas.harvard.edu/blog/september-kings-speech.
6. "Jefferson's Autobiography," Yale Law School, The Avalon Project, http://avalon.law.yale.edu/19th_century/jeffauto.asp.
7. "Journals of the Continental Congress—Petition to the King; July 8, 1775," Yale Law School, The Avalon Project, http://avalon.law.yale.edu/18th_century/contcong_07-08-75.asp.
8. "Jefferson's Autobiography."
9. Edmund Burke to Arthur Lee, August 22, 1775, in Richard Henry Lee, *Life of Arthur Lee* (Boston: Wells and Lilly, 1829), 43.
10. Lee, *Life of Arthur Lee*, 45.
11. Lee, *Life of Arthur Lee*, 45.

12. "Proclamation of Rebellion: August 23, 1775," Britannia Historical Documents, http://www.britannia.com/history/docs/procreb.html.
13. "King George III's Address to Parliament, October 27, 1775," Presentations and Activities, Library of Congress, http://www.loc.gov/teachers/classroom materials/presentationsandactivities/presentations/timeline/amrev/shots /address.html.

CHAPTER ELEVEN

1. King George III to Lord North, January 31, 1778, *The Correspondence of King George the Third with Lord North from 1768 to 1783*, ed. W. Bodham Dunne (London: John Murray, 1867), 125.
2. Samuel B. Griffith, *The War for American Independence* (Champaign, University of Illinois Press, 2002), 469.
3. Andrew Jackson O'Shaughnessy, *The Men Who Lost America* (New Haven, Conn.: Yale University Press, 2014), 30.
4. King George III to Lord North, February 9, 1778, *The Correspondence of King George the Third*, 133.
5. King George III to Lord North, February 9, 1778, *The Correspondence of King George the Third*, 133.
6. King George III to Lord North, February 9, 1778, *The Correspondence of King George the Third*, 133.
7. King George III to Lord North, March 13, 1778, *The Correspondence of King George the Third*, 148.
8. Dr. Robert V. McNamee, "Who Were the Carlisle Commissioners? Part One," *OUPblog*, August 19, 2013, https://blog.oup.com/2013/08/carlisle-commission -us-congress-part-1.
9. "From George Washington to John Banister, 21 April 1778," *Founders Online*, National Archives, last modified June 13, 2018, https://founders.archives.gov /documents/Washington/03-14-02-0525. Original source: *The Papers of George Washington*, Revolutionary War Series, vol. 14, *1 March 1778–30 April 1778*, ed. David R. Hoth (Charlottesville: University of Virginia Press, 2004), 573–79.
10. "Response to British Peace Proposals, Continental Congress, June 13, 1778," TeachingAmericanHistory.org, http://teachingamericanhistory.org/library /document/response-to-british-peace-proposals.
11. King George III to Lord North, August 12, 1778, *The Correspondence of King George the Third*, 207.
12. King George III to Lord North, August 12, 1778, *The Correspondence of King George the Third*, 207.
13. King George III to Lord North, March 7, 1780, *The Correspondence of King George the Third*, 310.

14. Professor Arthur Burns, "The Abdication Speech of King George III," Royal Collection Trust, January 2017, https://www.royalcollection.org.uk/collection /georgian-papers-programme/the-abdication-speech-of-george-iii#/ _ftnref100.
15. Dr. A. O'Donnell, "America Is Lost!," Royal Collection Trust, January 2017, https://www.royalcollection.org.uk/collection/georgian-papers-programme /america-is-lost.
16. George III, "Letter on the loss of America written in the 1780s precise year unknown," Royal.uk, https://www.royal.uk/sites/default/files/media/georgeiii .pdf.
17. "From John Adams to John Jay, 2 June 1785," note 17, *Founders Online*, National Archives, last modified June 13, 2018, founders.archives.gov/documents /Adams/06-17-02-0078. Original source: *The Adams Papers*, Papers of John Adams, vol. 17, *April–November 1785*, ed. Gregg L. Lint, C. James Taylor, Sara Georgini, Hobson Woodward, Sara B. Sikes, Amanda A. Mathews, and Sara Martin (Cambridge, Mass.: Harvard University Press, 2014), 134–45.
18. "From John Adams to John Jay, 2 June 1785," note 17.

CONCLUSION

1. "Address at Independence Hall," ed. Roy P. Balser, *The Collected Works of Abraham Lincoln*, National Park Service, last updated April 10, 2015, https://www.nps .gov/liho/learn/historyculture/independence-hall.htm.
2. "Peoria Speech, October 16, 1854," ed. Roy P. Balser, *The Collected Works of Abraham Lincoln*, National Parks Service, last updated April 10, 2015, https://www.nps.gov/liho/learn/historyculture/peoriaspeech.htm.
3. Collected Works of Abraham Lincoln, vol. 2, Lincoln, Abraham, 1809–1865. https://quod.lib.umich.edu/l/lincoln/lincoln2/1:526?rgn=div1;view=fulltext.
4. "Address at Independence Hall," ed. Roy P. Balser, *The Collected Works of Abraham Lincoln*, http://www.abrahamlincolnonline.org/lincoln/speeches /philadel.htm.

INDEX

INDEX